THE SHAMANIC DRUM

A GUIDE TO SACRED DRUMMING

by

Michael Drake

Talking Drum Publications
Bend, Oregon

Talking Drum Publications
PO Box 1846
Bend, Oregon 97709

Cover design and art by Elisia Drake

Library of Congress Catalog Card Number: 91-90824

ISBN 0-9629002-0-6

First Printing July 1991
Second Printing December 1991

Printed in the United States of America by
Maverick Publications, Inc.
P. O. Box 5007
Bend, Oregon 97708

DEDICATION:
This book is dedicated to the Earth Keepers:
May they renew the Sacred Hoop.

CONTENTS

Acknowledgments

Special thanks to:

My wife Elisia for her loving support and for walking beside me on the Medicine Wheel of Life.

Kathy Wedeking for typing the manuscript.

Douglas R. Ward, spiritual teacher, healer, and visionary, for illuminating the path and showing me the way.

Rudy Clements, tribal leader of the Confederated Tribes of Warm Springs, for sharing the teachings and ceremonies of his people.

Hopi elder Thomas Banyacya for sharing the ancient wisdom of his people. His strong stance on environmentalism, his service to communities and nations, and his reverence for the traditions and teachings of his people are an inspiration. Hearing his message was a blessing. Drumming for him was a powerful and joyful experience. Repeal PL 93-531.

Brooke Medicine Eagle, Earth Keeper, teacher, and great-great grandniece of Chief Joseph, the Nez Perce holy man and leader, for her encouragement and recommendations.

Patty "Flaming Star" Ledbetter, Cherokee Medicine Woman and Chief of the Lumbee Beaver Clan, for calling this lost Cherokee home.

Sun Bear, Chippewa Medicine Man and Earth Keeper, for his profound vision, teachings, and support.

Bear That Walks, Seneca Spirit Shaman, for his teachings and the sacred power object he passed on to me.

And finally, to Jade Wah'oo, traditional Shaman of Mongolian heritage, for keeping with his intent to make accessible to all peoples, regardless of bloodline, the knowledge and practice of "The Ways of Shamanism".

SONG OF THE DRUM

My drum has many voices.
My drum tells many stories.
This drum is full of mystery.
This drum is full of dreams.

Listen to the drum beat.
Listen to the heart beat.
Now you hear the hoof beat.
Now you hear the wing beat.
All are One.

Cherokee

Introduction

There is a great renewal of interest in the practice of shamanism. This surge of interest can in large part be attributed to the purity of shamanic cosmology as well as the freedom and individuality of the shamanic experience. No intermediary such as the church or priesthood is needed to access personal revelation and spiritual experience. All dimensions of reality and the mystical knowledge and powers they contain are available to one who practices shamanism. Every shaman becomes his or her own teacher, priest, and prophet. Shamanic practice brings one ultimate power over one's own life and the power to help others do the same.

A shaman is one who enters an altered state of consciousness, usually induced by drumming, in order to make journeys into alternate realities, seeking the knowledge and power indigenous to those worlds. Shamans utilize this knowledge and power to achieve and maintain the health of themselves and their communities. These ancient shamanic methods have withstood the tests of time, varying little from culture to culture. Over thousands of years of trial and error, primal peoples the world over developed the same basic principles and techniques of shamanic power and healing. A whole way of life evolved in which everything is based on being in relationship. All life forms in nature are interconnected and dependent. If one species suffers, all others are affected. The health and well being of humanity is dependent upon the overall health of the Earth's ecosystem. The shaman is sensitive to this sacred interrelationship and serves as an intermediary between nature and the community. The shaman's prayerful communion with the natural elements and powers preserves an orderly, harmonious universe. The shaman seeks harmony with nature and the drum serves as an instrument of attunement.

Introduction

Decades of intensive anthropological studies in shamanic cultures have yielded great insights into shamanic methodology, mythology, and cosmology, but relatively little has been revealed regarding the drum. To a certain extent, researchers have overlooked, misunderstood, and underestimated the drum's role in shamanic work. In addition, the "medicine" of drumming, like that of many spiritual matters and rituals has, until recently, been a closely guarded secret. Until 1978, with the passing of the American Indian Religious Freedom Act, it was illegal for Native Americans to practice their traditional religions in the United States. Past oppression has most certainly left traditional native peoples reticent about sharing spiritual doctrines.

Due to escalating environmental poisoning and nuclear militarism, concerned shamans and medicine people have, in recent years, shared their sacred teachings with non-native people. The intention is to teach individuals how to renew and maintain harmony with their families, communities, nations, and Earth herself. The hope is to restore a sense of sacred to the world, of the divinity present in nature and all living things—values that oppose exploitation of natural and human resources. The primal nature has never been fully integrated into the collective consciousness of humanity, but primal peoples are now sharing it. Sacred drumming is a significant part of the learning.

In Western culture, most people will never have the opportunity to meet a shaman, let alone learn from one. Though no substitute for an apprenticeship situation, a handbook can convey the fundamental methodological information. The information presented here represents the shamanic drum ways I learned under the tutelage of traditional Mongolian shaman Jade Wah'oo; the teachings of traditional Native Americans; as well as research data that I have collected over the past ten years. Truly significant shamanic knowledge can only be acquired through individual experience, however, one must first acquire the methods in order to utilize them. Shamanic drumming techniques are fundamental and essential to growth. Anthropologist Michael Harner, in his excellent book, *The Way of the Shaman: A Guide to Power and Healing*, observes that "the repetitive sound of the drum is usually fundamental to undertaking shamanic tasks ... "[1]

Shamanic drum ways provide the opportunity to acquire shamanic experiences. These ways do not require faith nor changes in your definition of reality. No change in your subconscious mind is required either, for the drum only awakens what is already there. It will awaken the shaman that is dormant within you. The primal rituals and symbolism of shamanism are of an archetypical nature. They are a part of our psyche—a part of you whether you choose to become aware of it or not.

The most effective way to learn shamanism is to adopt the same basic concepts shamans do. For example, when I speak of "power", it is primarily because the term is basic to shamanism. Power can represent many different things. To some shamans, power is understanding energy and how to utilize it. To others, it is a measure of one's ability to manifest a vision in the material world. However, it is best to avoid any preoccupation with seeking a scientific understanding of what power may really represent or why shamanism works. I practice shamanism myself, not because I understand why it works, but simply because it does work.

A SHAMAN'S MAGIC SONG

You Earth,
Our great Earth!
See, oh see:
All these heaps
Of bleached bones
And wind-dried skeletons!
They crumble in the air,
The mighty world,
The mighty world's
Air!
Hey-hey-hey!

Netsilik Eskimo

CHAPTER 1

The Role of the Drum

The drum has a role of first importance to the shaman, for its rhythm develops a oneness of feeling and purpose with the rhythms of the universe. Everything in the universe, from the smallest subatomic particle to the largest star, vibrates with rhythmic motion. Rhythm is the heartbeat of life. The drum's beat unites the shaman with all life forms into a single being, a single heartbeat. The drum reconciles all of the diverse and discordant aspects or elements of nature. It promotes individual and planetary resonance and restores harmony and balance.

The drum's sonorous voice expresses the basic rhythm patterns man has observed over and over in nature: the changing seasons, the tides, the heartbeat—life and death itself. Rhythm is a universal language. We respond to rhythm whenever we sense it and seek it out when it is not present for it is invariably pleasant.

Drumming affects aurally generated emotion more than any other instrument. Drum rhythms cover the whole range of human feeling. Whatever the emotion, the drum seems to compensate and offer satisfying expression. Drumming provides solace, relief from anger, courage when afraid, or even ecstasy.

Ecstasy is defined as a mystic, prophetic, or poetic trance. It is a trancelike state of exaltation in which the mind is fixed on what it contemplates or conceives. The drum acts as a focusing device for the shaman. It creates an atmosphere of concentration, enabling the shaman to sink into a light-trance state. It is an inward spiritual journey of joy and rapture in which the shaman performs his or her mysterious work.

The ecstatic experience does not belong exclusively to the shaman, but "is a timeless primary phenomenon."[1] All people, therefore, are capable of flights of rapture. Ecstasy is a frequency within each of us. Like tuning a radio to the desired frequency, the drum attunes one to ecstasy.

Shamanism has been defined as a technique of ecstasy. It is a great emotional and mental adventure open to any who wish to transcend their normal, ordinary definition of reality. The shaman is able to contact and utilize an ordinarily hidden reality in order to acquire knowledge, power, and to help others. He or she gains access to a whole new world, and yet familiarly mythical universe.

The mythology and creation stories of all Earth peoples speak of a primordial, but now lost paradise—a "Garden of Eden" in which humanity lived in harmony with all that existed. The cosmos had total access to itself. There was but one language for all creatures and elements. Humans were able to converse with animals, birds, minerals, and all living things. Animal characters, for example, played a prominent role in mythology. They were often portrayed as essentially human in bodily makeup, but possessed the individual characteristics of animals as they exist in nature today. Thus Coyote is distinguished in the tellings by its cunning, yet mischievous behavior, and Eagle by its great vision and ability to fly high into the realm of the Great Spirit.

Within the mythical paradise there existed a balanced union between the physical and the spiritual realms. Humans were aware that the spirit and ego are two manifestations of the same presence—that each human body is the manifestation of a spirit being on the material plane. Each human utilized the input of their intuitive and imaginative frequencies, the inner communication channels designed to maintain harmonious communion between each spirit and its physical human projection.

The imagination as a means of communication developed much earlier than language and used different neural pathways for the transmission of information. This preverbal imagery was both personal and transpersonal. On a personal level the imagination affected one's own physical health and well being. Images communicated with tissues and organs, even cells, to effect a change. Imagery was transpersonal in that it could be transmitted from the consciousness of one person to the corporeal structure of another. Intuition served as a conductor of divine knowing energy, thus each human received spiritual guidance from the "Creator" and played an active role in the continuing work of creation within the physical realm. Through the eyes of the soul (intuition) the Creator's actions appeared within human awareness as the most natural thing to do. Following their intuitive sense connected humans with the awesome powers of the universe. It connected the consciousness of one being to another, uniting the universe and its life forms completely.

As the centuries passed, humans began to place more emphasis on the input of their five physical channels of perception, forgetting that perception was also available to them on the more subtle imaginative and intuitive levels. With increasing emphasis on the physical, humans lost contact with their spiritual nature. In time, the body and its physical priorities became their sole reality. The harmonious bonding of the spirit/ego ceased to exist. Humans saw the spirit as separate from the physical body, their egos thereby cut them off from spiritual inner direction.

Without the communication systems designed to connect humans with creation, the Creator's plan (the "Sacred Vision") was left unfulfilled. Ego-humans departed into worlds of illusion dominated by fear, emotional turbulence, and warfare. Man's alienation from nature caused him many ills. He fell out of rhythm with life and ceased to grow.

Though the mythical paradise is lost in our physical mode of perceptual awareness, it still remains accessible along the intuitive and imaginative frequencies. In our day, as in times past, the shaman utilizes the drum to gain access into the mythical realm of reality. Through the drum's rhythms he or she transcends time and space to reestablish communication between the spiritual and the physical realms.

Altered States of Consciousness

The drum's pulse synchronizes the left and right hemispheres of the brain. When these hemispheres begin to pulsate in harmony, there is a change in the actual physiology of the brain waves that produces a heightened awareness. The awareness is expanded into the ecstatic state—the divine octave of resonance. With the divine frequency attuned, access to multidimensional increments of knowledge and wisdom is gained. These realities are then utilized as tools in this dimension. In this way the shaman creates a bridge, linking the Earth and sky—the spiritual realm above and the physical realm below.

The ethereal rainbow, arching high into the heavens symbolizes this harmonious union of body and soul. In her book *Voices of Our Ancestors: Cherokee Teachings From the Wisdom Fire*, Dhyani Ywahoo states: "We are the Rainbow, each of us. When we (the Cherokee) speak of rebuilding the Rainbow Bridge, it is to bring again into harmony the left and right hemispheres of the brain, to renew the flow of our intuitive mind ... "[2] Regarding the drum, she states: "Chanting and drumming were also a significant part of the learning, balancing activity of the right and left hemispheres of the brain ... "[3]

The left hemisphere of the brain functions primarily through a linear flow of information; the sequential process of analysis; and a continual referral to our past experiences stored in memory. The left cerebral specializes in science, mathematics, and language processing. It is characterized as deductive, rational, and producing consciousness.

The right hemisphere is involved primarily in processing visual and spatial information. Artistic, musical, and creative abilities are heavily dependent on right brain functions. The right cerebral is characterized as intuitive, imaginative, and the seat of the subconscious.

Each hemisphere is associated with opposite sides of the body, yet both sides complement each other. For example, "the right hemisphere (left ear) specializes in the perception of melody, pitch, timbre, and harmony, but there is a left-hemispheric (right ear) advantage pertaining to the perception of rhythm."[4] Most striking, however, is the right cerebral's ability to analyze or devour information all at once while the left hemisphere analyzes information one bit at a time. It is the right hemisphere that accesses the invisible sea of information that we bathe in daily—the all pervading frequencies of consciousness immanent in all phenomena. The right hemisphere accesses this intelligent energy primarily at a subconcious level. We become consciously aware of this information only when the two hemispheres are synchronized in harmony. The divine, creative, knowing energy can then flow unimpeded into our conscious awareness. The left cerebral allows us to see only the surface of things. Until the right side is awakened, "seeing" with the inner vision is not possible. Each person has the ability to connect directly with this energy/information flow, and can thus awaken to one's higher mind. Drumming rebuilds the "Rainbow Bridge".

Research has demonstrated that rhythmic drumming induces altered states of consciousness by activating electrical activity in "many sensory and motor areas of the brain, not ordinarily affected, through their connections with the sensory area being stimulated".[5] Drumming stimulates auditory driving or stimulation of cerebral electrical rhythms not ordinarily employed in the brain in normal conscious awareness. Drumming stimulates the rhythms of vision. Furthermore, the drum beat frequency determines the depth of the trance state. For example, drum beat frequencies in the theta wave EEG frequency range (four to seven cycles per second) induce corresponding theta brain wave rhythms. Theta brain activity is associated with drowsiness and a deep trance state.

Similarly, an alpha level drum frequency (seven to thirteen cycles per second) stimulates an alpha wave cycle in the brain. High alpha states are associated with meditation and holistic modes of consciousness. The alpha rhythm is the primary frequency produced by Earth's electromagnetic field. The 10-hertz band (10 cycles per second) is the primary frequency in all animals. All life pulsates in time to the Earth.

When the brain oscillates in this common frequency, attunement to the universal energy/information frequency is achieved.

By adjusting the tempo of drumming, the shaman controls the nature of the trance state. The shamanic state of consciousness, however, is dominated by the alpha wave cycle. In this light trance state, "part of the shaman's consciousness is usually still lightly connected to the ordinary reality of the physical or material environment where he is located".[6] This permits full recall later of the visionary experience, unlike the much deeper trance characteristic of mediumistic trance, psychedelic drug induced states, or hypnosis. The shaman maintains conscious control over the direction of travel, but does not know what mysteries will be uncovered. The experience is ecstatic—he or she is inspired and visionary.

The visionary experience is as valid as the ordinary state of consciousness. The basis for the empirical definition of reality is, after all, what is observed with one's own senses. Perception is the latticework of reality. The Australian anthropologist A.P. Elkin regarded the shamanic vision as "no mere hallucination. It is a mental formation visualized and externalized, which may even exist for a time independent of its creator... "[7]

The trance or transcendent state of awareness becomes a learned state of awareness through repeated journeys of the spirit into the mythical planes of reality. There the shaman learns to communicate with plants, animals, and the guiding spiritual forces of nature. He or she accesses knowledge, power, healing, and a harmonious union of the spirit/ego. He or she becomes a direct participant in the evolution of creation. The shaman, like our modern physical scientists, views the universe as a web of inseparable energy patterns that is in a continuous act of creation. By utilizing the input of the intuitive and imaginative energy frequencies, the shaman becomes the primary creative dynamic in the human realm.

SPIRIT SONG

As a head only, I roll around.
I stand on the rim of my nest.
I am enveloped in flames.
What am I? What am I?
I, the song, I walk here.

Modoc

CHAPTER 2

The Cosmology of the Drum

Humans have always looked beyond the factual world of ordinary reality for something solid on which to ground their lives. The models of the mystery of life have always been based on the myths of an immemorial imagination. "Mythological cosmologies do not correspond to the world of gross facts but are functions of dreams and visions."[1] Dreams and visions have always, and always will be the creative forces that shape cosmology. It is an inherent product of the psyche—a symbolic language of metaphysics recognized by shamans and seers. The personal vision of the shaman becomes the collective vision of the group.

Mythological cosmology is evocative rather than referential. It is not science or history, but rather symbolism that serves as a catalyst of spiritual well being. Like the beat of the shaman's drum, it disengages the individual from the integrating component of ordinary thinking consciousness and invokes the mysteries of the imagination and intuition. The realm of cosmology and the domain of shamanic trance are one and the same.

Nick Black Elk, the Sioux visionary and keeper of the sacred pipe, speaks of the drum's cosmology in his account of the seven sacred rites of the Oglala Sioux: "The drum is sacred. Its round form represents the whole universe, and its steady beat is the pulse, the heart, throbbing at the center of the universe. It is the voice of Wakan Tanka (the Creator), and this sound stirs us and helps us to understand the mystery and power of all things."[2]

The Ojibwa people believe that the drum represents the world. The drummers surround the drum just as the various spirit helpers of the Creator surround the world. The drum-

27

mers believe they are representing or "sitting in for" the Creator's spirit helpers. The drummers serve as a conduit for the words and knowledge of the divine source. The Ojibwa often refer to the drum as "our grandfather" (Creator). To attend a drum meeting is called "going to talk with grandfather".

This direct communication is made possible by the very structure of the universe. According to the primal cosmological concept, there are three great cosmic regions: the sky, the Earth, and the lowerworld. They are linked together by a great central axis which is commonly referred to in mythology as the world's tree, pillar, bridge, or stairway. The Mongol peoples call it the Golden Pillar and perched atop it is the Eagle. They perceive the stars as a herd of horses and the Pole Star (the top of the Golden Pillar) is the stake to which they are tethered. A tree of seven branches with a bird or eagle at its top is symbolism often found on prehistoric monuments. Its roots touch the underworld and its branches hold up the celestial canopy, with the Pole Star resting atop it. The World Tree is the road to the celestial supreme being. It is the umbilical cord of the universe, linking both the individual and the planet to the divine source. It rises from the Earth's "umbilicus" and represents the universe in a continuous act of creation.

Through the sound of the drum, the shaman is transported to the World Tree and is conveyed up or down a tube or tunnel that opens out upon bright and marvelous landscapes. The shaman can ascend to the sky realm of divine intelligence or make healing journeys to the underworld of death and rebirth to restore beneficial or vital power to a patient. By undertaking the ecstatic journey the shaman experiences communication among the cosmic zones.

The two-headed skin drum is preferred for shamanic work, for it constitutes a microcosm of the universe (See Appendix D, The Single-headed Drum). One side of the drum produces a higher tone and is connected to the sky or celestial realm. It generates an electrical energy that is positive, masculine, yang, and projective in nature. Electrical energies are

28

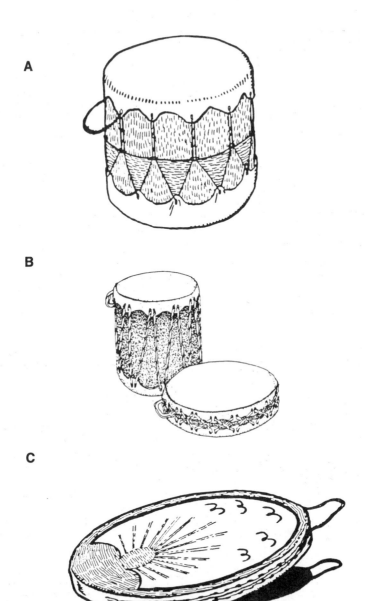

Two-headed drums:
(A) Apache; (B) Taos; (C) Chippewa.

ascending forces that carry consciousness into higher realms of divine knowledge.

The celestial side of the drum is often associated with the mythological Eagle that is perched atop the World Tree. Eagle will carry the shaman's prayers for higher knowledge and guidance to the divine source, or the shaman may transform into Eagle and soar into the celestial realm. The shaman and Eagle are both intercessors between the Creator and human beings. In mythology, Eagle is often associated with the origins of shamans.

The opposite side of the drum produces a deeper tone and is connected to the underworld. It generates a magnetic energy that is negative, feminine, yin, and receptive in nature. Magnetic energies are descending forces conducive to great healing, mind, and creative powers. Descents to the lower-world are often undertaken to find and return a sick person's vital power or wandering spirit. One who is sick is generally regarded as dis-spirited.

The underworld side of the drum is often linked to the archetypal Horse of mythology. The monotonous rhythm of shamanic drumming is suggestive of a horse on a journey. It is "... the exalted, buoyant state that one mounts and rides into the plane of enlightenment".[3] The shaman will ride Horse into the underworld on journeys of power or direct Horse to carry the beneficial power and healing to where it is needed.

The rim of the drum is connected to Earth as well as the mythical World Tree. The shell of the shaman's drum is often constructed of wood derived from a sacred tree. Like the World Tree which rises from the navel of Mother Earth, the rim of the drum links together the two sides (upper and lower realms) of the drum in perfect harmony. It unites the physical and the spiritual.

The two-headed drum restores the balance between masculine and feminine energy. This equilibrium is symbolized in the Nepali shamanic drum: "... there was a female and a male face to a dhyagro (drum) that was placed on a long carved handle ... The male side is painted with twenty white triangles representing the balance of the male and the female all along the edge".[4] The drum serves as an equilibrator, whose function is to reconcile all the diverse and contradictory aspects or elements of nature. This is also the function of the universe, and the drum is designed as its microcosm.

Life-force

The drum unites masculine and feminine energies, generating the force that bonds the atomic world together.[5] This vital "life-force" is the stick-em that holds life together. It is not molecular, not matter, but the pure source energy that structures our souls. This primordial force of life is the "will" or intention to be. "Will is the underlying current, the fire that brings forth that which we perceive as our reality."[6]

We tend to shut down the flow of this divine energy. Negative attitudes, fear, and anxiety are mind sets that create blockage. Drumming quickens our frequencies so that we actually begin to spin off the slower vibrations of anger, guilt, and fear. The blockages are removed as we move into the ecstatic state of harmonic resonance with the divine will. The drummer is one who is flowing along the current of will. The shamanic drummer is aligned with will, the voice of the Creator, the fundamental sound underlying all manifestation. The drummer thus becomes an instrument of creation in the material world.

The cosmology of the two-headed drum corresponds to the two primary functions of shamanism—the quest for knowledge and the accumulation of power. The celestial (male/electric) side of the drum tends to develop the capacity for inner vision and divine intuitive consciousness. This is development of the third eye or medicine eye, and higher energy centers or "chakras". (See Appendix B on Chakras)

The underworld (female/magnetic) side of the drum is the power side. It cultivates life energy force in the lower energy centers (chakras) of the body which is then stored in the area of the solar plexus. This energy can then be directed back to the higher energy centers of the intuitive mind or towards healing and creative endeavors. Divine knowledge is re-

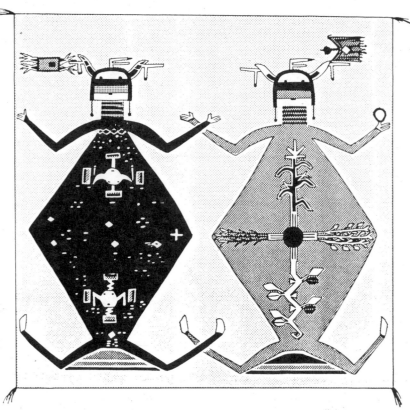

This Navajo rug depicts the motif of Mother Earth and Father Sky. The reproductive powers of the four elements which are sealed within the feminine structure of the Earth Mother (figure on the right) are united with the opposite polarity of Father Sky (figure on the left) to create life-force.

ceived from the upper realm and that knowledge is then empowered and directed through the lower realm.

Transformations of Myth Through Time

The mythical cosmology of the drum and of shamanism itself represents the world view of paleolithic hunting societies. The archetypal symbolism developed from a reciprocal relationship that existed between animals hunted and the tribal cultures dependent for sustenance on their offering themselves. The totemic animals or animal archetypes of vision are themselves great teachers and shamans, as well as man's co-descendants from the mythical paradise. The totemic animals gave to humans the rites to be performed when they (animals) had been slain so that their spirits would return to the source for rebirth. The hunt itself was a rite of sacrifice. When the rites were properly performed and recognition thus given to the mystery of the order of nature, then harmony with nature was maintained and a food supply assured.

The mythical cosmology of hunting (shamanic) cultures served a dual function. It engaged the individual both emotionally and intellectually in the local tribe, but also served as a means of disengaging from this local system in order to experience the "Great Mystery". The emphasis was on the individual—of breaking free and discovering one's own uniqueness, so as to bring something new back to the group.

The structures of shamanic cultures are circular. Like the hoop of the drum, the circle represents harmony and balance. All are equal in the circle—no one is above or below. In a circle, each person's face can be seen, each person's voice can be heard and valued. (see Appendix C)

Agriculture transformed the structures and cosmologies of shamanic cultures. Nomadic, subsistence hunting societies were assimilated into food growing communities structured on hierarchy. The Neolithic order of agricultural societies imposed a rigid social system on Paleolithic peoples used to the freedom and rites of the hunt. The plant displaced the animal as the model of the mysteries of life. Complex ceremonials and rituals based on the cycle of death and rebirth in the plant kingdom rigidly interlocked all individuals into the endless formal procedure. Shamans, with their individualistic style of spiritual experience, were viewed as a threat to the dogma of the ecclesiastical hierarchies. Shamanism was discredited as heresy and replaced by a socially anointed priesthood.

The paramount function of mythical cosmology in agricultural societies has always been that of suppressing individualism. Generally, this has been achieved by imposing dogmatic archetypes of behavior, symbols, and belief systems on people. Individual expression, interests, or modes of experience contrary to the social mandala are discouraged. In

1892, for example, Native American shamans were called "an influence antagonistic to the rapid absorption of new customs ... Only after we have thoroughly routed the medicine men from their entrenchments and made them an object of ridicule can we (whites) hope to bend and train the minds of our Indian wards in the direction of civilization."[7] The cultural imprinting of hierarchical, agriculturally based societies leaves the individual outside the realm of personal spiritual experience. Any sense of the "Great Mystery" is beyond the individual's grasp.

Today, the mythologies of hierarchy and the priesthood are dissolving. Individuals are searching for new ways to relate to nature and spirituality. "What is required of us all, spiritually as well as corporeally, is much more the fearless self-sufficiency of our shamanistic inheritance rather than the timorous piety of the priest-guided Neolithic."[8]

The cosmology of the shaman's drum is one of disengagement from the rigid patterns that suppress the manifestations of individualism. Through the beat of the drum, a sense of the divine source (upperworld) is evoked, along with the forces of the universe which have been chained in the subliminal abyss of the subconscious (underworld) for six thousand years. We participate directly in the work of encountering and transforming our inner structure which mirrors our culture. Structure determines how energy will flow, where it will be directed, and what new forms and structures will be created. Through the transformation of our inner landscapes, we transform the external landscapes. We create new forms, new structures, not based on hierarchy, estrangement, and exploitation. We renew the sacred hoop of harmony and balance. This is the work of the shaman—of myth-making.

SHAMAN'S DRUM

Oh! My many-colored drum
Ye who standeth in the forward corner!
Oh! My merry and painted drum,
Ye who standeth here!
Let thy shoulder and neck be strong.

Hark, oh hark my horse—ye female maral deer!
Hark, oh hark my horse—ye bear!
Hark, oh hark ye!

Oh, painted drum who standeth in the forward
corner!
My mounts—male and female maral deer.
Be silent sonorous drum,
Skin-covered drum,
Fulfill my wishes.

Like flitting clouds, carry me
Through the lands of dusk
And below the leaden sky,
Sweep along like wind
Over the mountain peaks!

Soyot (Tuvas) of Siberia

CHAPTER 3

The Fundamentals of Shamanic Drumming

The potential is unlimited, yet the fundamentals of shamanic drumming are relatively simple:

1. Always begin by making smoke offerings. You should burn sage, sweetgrass, cedar, or tobacco. Smoke offerings clarify and purify mind and environment. Smudge yourself by drawing the smoke first over your heart, then over the top of your head, purifying body, mind, and spirit. Next smudge the drum, drumstick, and any other sacred objects by passing them through the smoke.

Smoke offerings carry one's prayers into all realms of existence. Pray to and invoke the primordial elements: Earth, Water, Fire, and Air. Pray to the Animal, Plant, and Mineral kingdoms. Praying not only invokes these powers, but also is a way of giving energy that helps these elements and kingdoms to continue to have harmony and balance. Turn to each of the four directions in a clockwise fashion, offering smoke and prayers. Invoke the powers of the East, the South, the West, and finally the North. Pray to Father Sky and Mother Earth.

When we stand in the place of power and pray to each direction, we are centering and bringing ourselves into balance. We are also creating a circle—a boundary that separates the sacred from the ordinary and profane. Such a ritual sets the trance state firmly apart from ordinary waking consciousness, makes it a separate territory that can be slipped in and out of at will. By creating a circle, we are also structuring an energy pattern that will contain, focus, and amplify the power generated by drumming. The circle also forms a barrier against the intrusion of unwanted forces. (See Appendix C, Medicine Wheel Of Life)

2. The next step is to ground yourself. Grounding means to root yourself, to connect with Earth. Grounding keeps the body linked to Earth and physical reality while the spirit journeys into alternate realities. It allows one to maintain a portion of ordinary awareness while experiencing non-ordinary awareness. It grounds the experience of expanded consciousness into physical reality, as well as grounding spiritual forces in the physical body.

Ground yourself by sitting with spine straight, still the mind, and breathe deeply from the belly to open the lower energy centers that ground us in physical reality. Through the breath Earth and Heaven meet. We draw Earth's energy up through the spine, and celestial energy down through the top of the head. The two meet at the heart and expand, radiating outward. Visualization will aid in the grounding process if you can imagine the spinal column as a tree—"The Cosmic Tree" or "Tree of Life". Visualize roots that extend from the root chakra deep into Earth. Visualize the spinal column as the trunk with branches rising up through the top of the head, reaching into the sky. Like the "World Tree", a conduit is formed, linking the individual and the planet to the divine source.

3. Once you are grounded, it is important to form your intent. "Intent is a universal, abstract force responsible for molding everything in the world we live in."[1] The intent is our will. Intent should be from the heart and specific. Your intent could be focused on anything. It may be for healing and enlightenment for yourself, someone else, or the planet. You could ask for the power to perform a healing. You could pray for the power to manifest your full potential, talents, and purpose, or simply ask for whatever divine guidance or knowledge you need at this time.

You may wish to manifest something or to influence events in the material world, however, you must be careful not to fall into the trap of sorcery. If you seek first the "Sacred Vision" of the Great Spirit, you will see as the Creator sees.

By aligning yourself with the will of the Creator you will find that what you need from the Earth Mother will come readily into your hands. However, if you seek first to secure your earthly desires and forget the spirit, you will block your own spiritual growth. The most deadly kind of sorcery is that which we unconsciously inflict on ourselves. Anger, fear, envy, greed, deceit, and self-degradation all manifest themselves as psychosomatic and stress related disorders. Pray for harmony and balance in your life.

4. Having formed your intent, the next step is to begin drumming, and always begin on the celestial (high tone) side of the drum.(See Appendix D, The Single-headed Drum). It is projective in nature and carries your prayers, intent, and consciousness into the celestial realm. If, for example, you seek divine guidance as to how to perform a healing, then drum with that intent. Close your eyes and focus your attention upon the beat of the drum. Move the drumstick around the head of the drum as you play, allowing the various tones and overtones of the song of creation to resonate through you. Thus, you are attuned to sacred harmony and wisdom. No particular tempo, rhythm, or pattern is required since different persons require a different tempo on different occasions. However, a rapid "eagle heartbeat" (180-200 beats per minute) is quite effective.

Work the drum to build up the hum of the overtones. These are the best frequencies for power, knowledge, and healing. Harmonic energy flows between the drumhead and the drumstick. That power (life-force or will) pulls and draws on the drumstick. Allow the drum to guide you.

The guidance or knowledge thus received may come through visions, symbols, or images. It may simply be an intuitive/knowing awareness. The intuitive feelings and impressions are generally of higher frequency than the visual information and, therefore, higher knowledge. However, it is not essential that you become cognizant or consciously aware of any particular guidance. Simply allow the drum (Eagle) to carry your prayers and intent into the celestial realm.

5. Once you have received divine guidance or knowledge, or when you sense intuitively that your prayers and intent have penetrated all dimensions and reached the Great Spirit, then begin drumming on the lowerworld (lower tone) side of the drum. You are now drawing this divine energy, knowledge, and consciousness down into the lowerworld to ground, empower, and/or direct it. If you are healing, then direct the source energy in the manner dictated by the visual or intuitive awareness received. Here again, if your intent is focused, you need not necessarily determine what needs healing within yourself, someone else, or within the Earth. Merely let the drum (Horse) do the healing. The drum will generate and direct the energy based solely on your intent and prayers.

6. Lastly, drum once again on the celestial side of the drum. Offer thanks to the Great Spirit for the blessings received. Offer thanks to Grandfather Sun and Grandmother Moon; to Father Sky and Mother Earth; to the powers of the four directions; to Eagle and Horse; and to "all my relations". The phrase "all my relations" ends many prayers in Native American tradition, for all living things share in the relationships of life on Earth. Offer prayers of love, compassion, and harmony. The drum (Eagle) will carry your prayers into all realms.

Harmonic Resonance

Sacred drumming generates harmonic resonance—a synchronization of two or more tones. It is the weaving of harmonic overtones that repairs the sacred tapestry of life. Fundamental harmonics of vibrational frequency waves structure our physical reality as well as alternate realities. Everything in the universe vibrates at a specific resonant frequency, which is an integral multiple of the voice of the Creator, the fundamental frequency, underlying all manifestation. A coherent cycle of frequencies is an octave and it is octaves of wave forms that structure matter. The structure of an atom can hold only eight electrons (an octave). The shell is complete and another expansion must occur in order to create a new shell or harmonic zone, which again fills up to a maximum of eight electrons. More and more complex structures are created through a repetition of octaves of wave forms. The universe is composed of a symphony of wave forms with the harmonics played on a vast range of octaves. All aspects of matter and reality can, therefore, be manipulated, altered, or transmuted resonantly as harmonic overtones.[2]

Work the drum so that it sings and hums. Synchronize your intent with these frequency overtones. Resonate with the divine octave of ecstasy.

Journeys

There may be some confusion as to what one should experience while drumming. The shamanic state of consciousness, like shamanism in general, is an individual experience. Some people may find they have a highly developed inner vision while others may rely more on instinct, intuition, or intent. It is an individual experience of a nonordinary reality and other shamans never challenge the validity of someone else's experiences.

Prevalent among the descriptions given of shamanic drum journeys is that of a tunnel or tube to which the shaman is transported. The tunnel sometimes appears ribbed and may bend or spiral around. This tunnel-like imagery is associated with the cosmological "World Tree", the central axis that links together the cosmic regions. It is the umbilical cord through which the shaman's spirit departs the physical body, and then returns in spiritual rebirth. The shaman is conveyed up or down the tunnel, often guided by a blue light, to an exit that opens out upon mysterious worlds. (It is interesting to note that such tunnel imagery is prevalent among descriptions given of the near-death experience.)

Journeys to the celestial or upperworld are made to acquire divine guidance and knowledge regarding the evolution of our universe. Journeys to the underworld are made to acquire great healing, mind, and creative powers. In these worlds the shaman experiences sensations and communications that go beyond the usual senses. Conversing with animals, plants, and other life forms becomes possible. Upon finishing the explorations, the shaman returns via the tunnel to ordinary reality.

During the journey, one's awareness transcends the ordinary reality of time, space, and body. In journeys to the underworld one may perceive and experience the sensation of falling, sliding, or spiraling downward into or under the Earth. In upperworld journeys one may perceive and experience the sensation of rising, floating, flying, or spiraling upward through the air or sky.

Journeys to the underworld involve the movement of awareness to a level beneath ordinary reality (the subconscious) and celestial journeys involve movement to a level higher than ordinary reality (divine consciousness). Lower levels are denser, lower in frequency, and more involved with the physical body, the earth plane, and physical reality. Higher levels are higher in frequency, less dense, and more subtle.

The colors you perceive on drum journeys are important for they often indicate what level of awareness you are experiencing and which chakra (see Appendix B) center you are activating. The chromatic hues correspond to the vibrational tones of each phase of ascending consciousness. They also correspond to the seven chakras and are from bottom to top: red, orange, yellow, green, blue, indigo, and violet. For example, if you enter a world of violet mountains, sky, or sun, you can assume that you have achieved one of the highest levels of awareness in the celestial realm. If you perceive more reds, oranges, and yellows, you are experiencing lowerworld levels of awareness.

Remember that nothing can harm you on your journeys without your permission. You can banish an offensive situation, spirit, or being from your vision, or simply return to ordinary reality. However, you should always be respectful of spirits in other realms. In addition, you can ask for gifts of power and/or knowledge from the spirit beings you encounter. The accumulation of shamanic power and knowledge comes primarily from journeys, visions, and dreams, or in other words, altered states. It would be advisable to record one's journeys in a journal as soon as one has returned to ordinary reality. Journeys, like dreams, tend to fade quickly from conscious awareness. Keeping a journal provides a record of one's spiritual growth and allows one to reflect upon and better interpret journeys.(See Appendix E to read accounts of journeys.)

Learning to leave the physical body is important, for without this experience, the spirit may become confused after death. The spirit may become lost between this world and the next. The spiritual death is one of the most important lessons for a shaman apprentice. It is a spiritual journey of the imagination and intuition. The shaman controls only the beginning and end of the journey. The shaman is carried away by the vision, creating and becoming the vision. Visions are the shaman's window to the spirit world.

The vision, however, is never the goal. The purpose of altering one's consciousness is to access the knowledge and power of other realities and to then utilize it in the physical realm to benefit the community. The goal is to expand one's awareness, to seek enlightenment, to accept the mystery of life and enter into it. Trust your intuition and inner vision, and have faith in your spiritual power.

Shamanic drumming enables us to transcend ordinary reality or the way we ordinarily perceive reality. The Quantum Theory states that our material world is created over and over before our very eyes each instant we perceive it. We can change reality just by changing the ways we perceive it. Our world is not real. It is a fantastic illusion of genetic and cultural imprinting. There is only energy—formless and infinite. We can't resist energy because we are energy. When we practice sacred drumming, we feel that primal energy. We become one with what we are made of.

POWER SONG

Oh spirits awaken with light,
On wings of the Eagle take flight.
Soar between the Earth and Sky,
And in Harmony unite with me.

From the Lowerworld you arise,
To bring me power and advise.
Ride the winds of the World's Rim,
Then descend to me at the Center.

Cherokee

CHAPTER 4

Power Practice

Power practice is fundamental to the maintenance of one's personal power and well being. One of the most crucial aspects of power practice in all shamanic cultures is the development of inner imagery and visions. In altered states shamans develop such vivid internal imagery that the awareness of ordinary perception and bodily sensations are blocked out. Once vivid life like imagery is experienced, the next phase of practice is to develop control over the internal imagery. By orchestrating the inner imagery, the shaman consciously interacts with the visionary content. In this way the shaman is able to contact spirit guides, power animals, and givers of power. Over a period of time the shaman develops the ability to see past, present, and future events. In these altered states the shaman accumulates knowledge and inner power, and is capable of influencing events for social benefit.

Visualization is a discipline that certain people have greater ease in mastering. Other people experience intuitive guidance without vivid internal imagery. Developing inner vision and visualization is a worthwhile endeavor for all people. What you see clearly is easier to manifest, for patterns of mind create reality. Visualization combined with sacred drumming creates a powerful renewing energy—the power of transformation.

Power Animals

Developing the capacity for inner vision in altered states allows one to connect with totemic guardian spirits. Guardian spirits such as Eagle, Coyote, and Bear represent and protect their entire species. The possessor of a guardian animal then draws upon the spiritual power of the entire species. Through the practice of finding and working with a power animal one reestablishes the spiritual communication and alliance that existed in mythical times. One connects with the animals, birds, fish, plants, and other beings of alternate realities. The power animal guides, protects, and can act as one's alter ego. Shamans often undergo a spiritual transformation from human to power animal, and back again.

Power animals represent an aspect of power and wisdom that a shaman must develop. In many cultures the teachings and knowledge received from one's power animal is considered more important than the practical guidance of a master shaman. Shamans may have up to two power animals connected to each of the chakras in the body, except for the crown. The crown chakra is reserved as the roost of the Eagle. One acquires the wisdom and vision of Eagle when one sees the future implications of one's actions. The power of the Eagle is to soar above the hurdles of life's dilemmas, keeping one's eyes focused on the "Sacred Vision". When one acquires a new power animal, the energy center associated with that animal becomes active.

The animal/human unity of the mythical past means that a person usually possesses one or more guardian spirits or power animals. Most shamanic cultures believe that one is born with a guardian spirit—that at the moment of birth, one's power animal is born in the wild. One may have several power animals over the course of a life time and never realize it. We long ago lost our ability to communicate with the elements and forces of nature. Shamans, on the other hand, frequently see, consult, and metamorphose into their guardian spirits. Without this unity, it is widely accepted that it is impossible to become a shaman. The shaman must have this spiritual power and guidance in order to master the spiritual powers of alternate realities.

Recognizing and acquiring one's own guardian spirit is of utmost importance in becoming a shaman. The most well-known method of acquiring a power animal is the vision

**Totemic Eagle rendered
from a Haida wooden drum.**

quest or vigil conducted in a remote wilderness location where one evokes the spirits through fasting and prayer. Another method is shamanic drumming. The Aborigines of Australia utilize the drum to connect with guardian spirits. They believe that the drumbeat reverberates around the mountain tops where the echo invokes the spirits existing in the cosmic zones around the mountain back to the physical world. You can also evoke or contact your guardian spirit through drumming. The guardian spirit can appear in either animal or human form, but most likely you will see or sense its animal aspects.

Within the mythical cosmology of the two-headed drum, "Eagle" and "Horse" represent intercessors between humans and the upper and lowerworlds. They are the guardians of these two realms. In a sense, they are the gate-keepers that open the crack between the worlds, allowing humans to once again experience these mythical realms. Your initial encounter with guardian spirits will most likely involve these two archetypal power animals. They may or may not be one of your personal guardian spirits, yet connecting with them reestablishes spiritual communication with the world of power animals. Though you may not initially possess Eagle or Horse as personal power animals, in time you may acquire them as such. Eagle and Horse can aid you in the process of acquiring your own guardian spirit based solely on your intent, for they are conveyers of intent.

Acquiring A Power Animal

1. After offering smoke, smudging, and grounding, begin drumming on the celestial side of the drum with your intent focused upon meeting and acquiring your guardian spirit. Here again, everyone's experience is unique, but you should eventually get some impression of what your power animal is. The spiritual guidance received may be intuitive or visual. The main thing at this stage is to keep your intent focused. Your intent and prayers will then be conveyed to all realms by Eagle.

2. When you intuitively sense that your prayers have reached the celestial realm or when you receive some impression of what your power animal is, then switch to the lowerworld side of the drum. The lowerworld side of the drum will draw your consciousness down into the realm of power animals, as well as magnetize and draw the animal to you. It is in this realm that your search begins. Search with your eyes closed and your intent focused on connecting with your power animal. Your power animal will enter your awareness visually or intuitively. Be open to the sensations and feelings of being that animal. You may see the nonordinary landscape or environment in which the animal exists. You may see the animal as well. Being and seeing the animal commonly happen simultaneously. You may sense other animals (such as Horse) or beings as well. The key to recognizing your guardian spirit is that it will enter your awareness visually or intuitively at least four times.[1] Avoid any menacing fanged reptiles, spiders, or spider webs. If you cannot pass around them, then simply return and try to journey on another occasion.

3. Once an animal has revealed itself to you four times, mentally welcome the animal to stay in your body—to unite in harmony with you. Now, return rapidly to ordinary reality. The animal will willingly return with you, otherwise it would not have revealed itself. Bring nothing else back with you on this journey.

4. Once you have returned to the physical realm, switch again to the celestial side of the drum to offer prayers of thanks.

Do not strain yourself to find or experience the guardian spirit. It will reveal itself only when it is ready and when you are ready. There is a right time and a right place for everything. You may have to drum on many different occasions before evoking your power animal. You may find the guardian spirit was an animal that you have always been attracted to or had an unusual experience with in the wild. In addition, it will not be a domesticated animal or an insect. It will generally be some kind of mammal, bird, or fish.

Guardian spirits are always beneficial. They are harmless, no matter how fierce they may appear to be. You possess the power animal; it can never possess you. The guardian spirit wants to experience once again living in material form within your body. In exchange, you experience the power of the whole genus of animals represented by the guardian as well as its nonordinary reality.

If, over a period of time, you fail to communicate and interrelate with your power animal, the unity may become weakened or severed. The power animal may wander, seeking a more harmonious alliance. Illness and disease may occur when one becomes "dis-spirited". A journey to retrieve the power animal may become necessary.

Use your guardian spirit in daily life by keeping consciously aware of how you feel. Sense it when you walk, exercise, and work. Recognize powerful omens, dreams, and visions as messages from the animal. Drum your power animal regularly. Consult and transform into it regularly on your drum journeys. You may even send your power animal to distant places to help or guide others (with their permission). Avoid sending your own energy in distant healing. Send the power of the guardian spirit instead.

What one gains or what one learns from a power animal is dependent upon one's self. The potential is limited only by the imagination, yet the imagination is infinite.

Synchronicities

Animals and birds in one's ordinary state of awareness can bring messages or guide you. The important thing is to notice it, and notice what it does. Nature is communicating with us all the time. Be aware of your surroundings. Look for synchronicities. They involve an internal psychological event that corresponds to an external observable event. Some aspect of a journey, vision, or dream may manifest in your ordinary reality. It is important to be on the lookout for the occurrence of synchronicities, for they offer confirmation that your personal power is producing effects far beyond the bounds of probability or coincidence.

Communicating With Nature

Developing communication with nature reconnects one to the natural elements of Earth, Water, Fire, and Air. These primal Earth forces are profoundly intelligent and understand the structure of matter and divine truth more comprehensively than humans do. These elemental forces are the building blocks of nature and interact with humans in the creative process. It is the blending of our thoughts and actions with the Earth and her forces that shape reality. Humans are the connecting link between the Divine Source and the forces of nature. We are the creative extensions of the Creator and nature awaits our guidance. Through sacred drumming we become a clear channel for the thoughts of the Creator. The world becomes our paint and canvas. This recognition is the cornerstone of the new "Sacred Reality".

A close interaction between humans and nature must be renewed. The increasing unpredictability of nature which manifests in dramatic climate swings, unsettled tides, tremors, and the like indicate that Earth's natural elements are confused and seek our harmonious guidance. Without nature's cooperation, humanity will cease to exist on this planet. Our existence is dependent upon forces that humanity subjugates and ignores. Nature can exist without humans, however, we cannot live without nature. Nature is searching beyond the human level for guidance. The Earth is a living being concerned with her own survival. Humans may find themselves obsolete on this planet. Evolution waits for no one.

Opening a line of communication is fundamental to interacting with nature. Communication with nature involves the imaginative and intuitive levels of perception. Sacred drumming expands and clarifies these frequencies of communication, linking the awareness of one being to another. Whenever two objects resonate in a harmonic vibratory state, energy is exchanged. Awareness is transmitted, life-force to life-force.

Everything that exists is imbued with life-force—intelligent energy.

The communication process goes as follows: Take your drum to an outdoor location that is preferably quiet and private. A wilderness or wild area away from the city is preferred, for nature is less encumbered with man's confusing thought patterns in such environments. Walk through the natural setting with the awareness that life-force communications with natural elements are possible and be open to such communication. You may be drawn to a particular plant, animal, insect, rock, mountain, or the like; or you may open a line of communication with the life-form of your choosing.

If, for example, you seek communion with a particular plant, then sit in silence near the plant. Make smoke offerings, smudge yourself and the drum, ground yourself and form your intent, which in this case is communication with the plant's spirit. Gaze at the plant and begin drumming on the celestial side of the drum. The mind is no longer in the body, but projected into the object of your gaze. After a few minutes, switch to the lowerworld side of the drum. Close your eyes and visualize the plant in your mind. This specific imagery serves as an invitation to the plant's life-force, literally drawing it to you. After creating a visual image of the plant, allow this image to fade away. This allows the plant to communicate in whatever form it wishes or deems appropriate. It may be visual, auditory, intuitive, or some combination of these. Communication may enter your awareness as a flash of color in your mind's eye, a visual symbol, a tingling of your spine, or the gentle touch of a breeze in your hair. You may even travel or be led through a tunnel to the lowerworld to encounter the spirit form of the plant which may appear in human form, as an animal, or possibly some mythical being. Work with these patterns of perception until a common dialogue can be defined. End the exercise with a round of drumming on the celestial side of the drum, offering prayers of thanks.

It may require numerous attempts before perceiving any contact. You are not accustomed to such communication, nor are the natural elements used to being summoned. As with

54

power animals, you may establish communication with a spirit (totemic) representative for the entire species. As you become more proficient, you can seek answers to specific questions or simply ask the spirit if it has any guidance for you at this time. Such open communication unites you with the natural elements. The rocks, the trees, the rivers, the mountains, and Earth have much to share.

Drumming Celestial Bodies

This communication can be extended beyond the elemental forces of the planet to the depths of the celestial realm. In Australia, for example, Aboriginal society practices sky gazing. By gazing at the sky, one's awareness is reflected out into the cosmos. The universe is imbued with infinite knowledge which can be learned. The planets, stars, and constellations influence our planet. Celestial and Earth energies meet within the human body. It is the responsibility of each individual to harmonize these energies and to resonate this vibration of harmony back into the universe.

Drumming celestial bodies is most beneficial for the planet and opens one's awareness to great knowledge and power. The sun, moon, planets, and stars have been the focus of ceremony and ritual since ancient times. The planet Venus, for example, is the mythical Goddess of Love. The Earth's sister planet is believed to be a source of benevolent and inspirational energy. The rhythms of sun and moon influence the Earth's internal energy. Lunar and solar currents generate biorhythm cycles within the planet. Sacred life energy flows within Earth's body as it does within our's. "Grandmother Moon" emanates feminine healing energy. "Grandfather Sun" is masculine in nature and serves as the solar system's central coordinator of the Creator's source energy. According to many ancient myths, Sirius and the stars of the Pleiades emanate the voice of the Creator. "These star systems give forth a crystal voice singing throughout all worlds."[2]

According to current astrophysics, density waves or galactic beams sweep through the galaxy and influence galactic evolution. "A cycle of several centuries is driven from some-where in the galactic core."[3] The source of this galactic intelligence is believed to be communicated by at least two star systems. One is Sirius, a star of the constellation Canis Major which is the brightest star and possibly the smallest and heaviest of all stars in the heavens. Our solar system appears to circle about Sirius in the latter's circuit of the Milky Way. Many believe this double-star to be the central star of all stars. According to Hopi cosmology, "Sirius, the Dog Star, is the star that controls the life of all beings in the animal kingdom".[4]

The Pleiades star cluster is a group of at least 300 stars within the constellation Taurus. Seven of these stars are most visible to the naked eye and are often referred to as "The Seven Sisters", "The Seven Dancers", or "The Harmonious Ones". Virtually all cultures have attributed great power and influence to these seven stars. "Canst thou bind the sweet influences of the Pleiades, or loose the bands of Orion?" Job 38:31. The seasonal behavior of the Pleiades was a sign of order in the cosmos. Many cultures trace their primeval home to the Pleiades star cluster and consider it to be the dwelling place of the Creator. These seven stars symbolize the seven universes or worlds through which humanity and Earth will evolve. These stars exist within each of us on a microcosmic level as the seven major chakras. The Seven Sisters and the seven chakras represent creation.

The seven principal stars of the constellation Ursa Major, called the Big Dipper, are the "Seven Brothers". They are related to the Seven Sisters. They are said to contain great knowledge. The star forming the outer end of the handle corresponds to the root chakra. This star, in particular, holds great healing power for Mother Earth.

Drumming and communion with celestial bodies should be reserved for more intermediate work. This level of power practice should only be pursued after one has acquired a power animal and developed spiritual communication and alliance with the elemental forces of nature. In order to serve as an efficient conduit of these celestial influences, you must attune and condition your resonant energy body. Approach power with power and with respect.

When you sense that your level of power and awareness has sufficiently developed, then practice this drumming exercise. On a clear night, choose an outdoor location that is secluded, open, and quiet. Sit comfortably and make smoke offerings to clarify and purify mind and environment. Smudge yourself, your drum, beater, and any other sacred objects. Ground yourself, form your intent, and from the heart. If, for example, you wish to draw stellar energy down to heal the planet, then make that your intent. Any of the celestial bodies previously mentioned could serve as the object of your focus. Some may be more difficult to locate than others. An astronomy book and a hand held planisphere would be most helpful.

Begin drumming on the celestial side of the drum, and raise your eyes to the star of your choosing. Offer prayers for knowledge and power to heal the planet. Your prayers and awareness will be projected to this star, the object of your focus. Move the drumstick or beater around the drumhead as you drum, seeking the knowledge and power of the different tones and overtones. Continue drumming for several minutes, allowing your awareness to merge with the vast awareness of this star.

Switch to the lowerworld side of the drum and close your eyes, focusing within upon your root chakra. Visualize the star and superimpose it over the area of your root chakra. This draws the knowledge and life-force down and grounds it within you and the planet. Continue to focus your attention inward upon the root chakra, but allow the image of the star to fade away. This allows the star to communicate and heal in whatever form it deems appropriate.

Finally, switch again to the celestial side of the drum, offering prayers of thanks for the celestial energy and blessings received. You are serving as a living conductor of stellar and galactic energy. Our souls, in fact, are composed of the same energy as the stars. The soul itself is a microcosm of the macrocosm (universe). From the stars we came and to the stars we shall return.

Protecting Yourself

Another aspect of power practice is to protect yourself from dark influences, energies, and people. If, for example, someone judges, ridicules, or threatens you, that discordant energy can harm you. Use the drum to protect yourself. Find sanctuary in a place where you feel secure and powerful. It may be your home, a mountain, or a place you hold sacred. Make smoke offerings and pray for harmony and balance. After smudging and grounding, begin drumming on the celestial side of the drum using a rapid eagle-heart beat (180-200 beats per minute). Focus on what that person has said to you—that statement or dark energy. Maintain a positive and grateful attitude that this person has cared enough to single you out—to honor you with their criticism or intimidation. Ask spirit Eagle to carry that negative energy high into the celestial realm to transform and transmute it.

When you sense that Eagle has transformed this dark energy, then switch to the lowerworld side of the drum. You are now magnetizing and drawing that transformed positive energy back down. Focus upon your root chakra and it will be grounded within you. End the drumming with a final round on the celestial side, offering prayers of thanks to Eagle and "all our relations".

That positive energy is now yours. This person has given you power. He or she may even become weakened or affected in some negative way due to this loss of power. If you should meet this person somewhere, do not confront them about the incident. Instead, be polite. Ask them how they are doing. They will have recognized their wrong-doing.

You should protect your drum from negative influences. Do not expose your drum to negative thoughts, words, or people. It is a sacred and should be treated as such.

Drumming Circles

The drumming circle is another method of power practice that should be explored. It provides the opportunity for people of like mind to join together in harmony. Simply join together, forming a circle, and then form your shared intent or goal. Group drumming is generally unison drumming, so individuals should alternate the responsibility of setting the tempo and leading the group. The drums draw individual energies together, unifying them into one powerful force. The group's power is equal to the square of the number of people in the group.[5] Ten individuals, sharing a common goal, would therefore have the power of one hundred individuals. Even a small group of people of one mind, one purpose, and fully attuned through the drums, can transform the world and manifest what is needed to benefit all beings.

Power practice keeps you clear, pure, and connected. Avoid becoming impatient if your powers do not develop as quickly as you would like. You must learn at your own pace. Accept life as you experience it and realize that there are many things you will never know. Accept the "Great Mystery". This acceptance helps one to more fully enjoy life's journey, and allows one to live more fully in the moment. Control of power gifts from alternate realities is a stepping-stone, not a street. Don't become enamored with the gifts, powers, or abilities acquired along the path, for these could become pitfalls or traps. Enlightenment should be your ultimate goal.

FROM THE NAVAJO MOUNTAIN CHANT

The voice that beautifies the land!
The voice above,
The voice of the thunder
Within the dark cloud.
Again and again it sounds,
The voice that beautifies the land!

Navajo

CHAPTER 5

Healing the Earth

Shamanic drumming can be used for different intents and purposes. The way of the healer, not of the sorcerer, is the way to health and harmony. It is important to never heal someone or to practice distant healing unless asked to do so. To treat someone without their permission would be sorcery. However, it is perfectly alright to offer healing to the Mother Earth. She is calling out to all for healing and for harmony. She is alerting us that now is the time to transform selfish actions and thought patterns to compassionate caretaking. Humans tend to perceive the Earth as a vast storehouse of natural resources—resources that are continually extracted with little regard to the well being of the planet and her rich diversity of life forms.

Many people today are sensitive to the suffering and degradation of Gaia. They are seeking a more holistic relationship with the planet. That is why so many are drawn to traditional Native American teachings, for they are primal and convey the sanctity and harmony of nature.

The sacred teachings from every tradition describe these times we are living in as an era of cleansing and purification for the planet. Healing the planet must begin with our own purification. We must make a conscious change in the ways we think and act. We must affirm peace, love, and harmony in every aspect of our lives. We must bring into balance the sacred currents of life.

Planetary Grid

Creative masculine and feminine energy currents connect and flow within everything that exists. In the human body, intuitive (masculine) celestial energy flows down the spine through the top of the head. Feminine Earth energy rises up through the navel. Sacred meridians carry these subtle energies throughout the body. We receive life-force currents from both Heaven and Earth and they both meet in the heart. From the heart, these combined energies expand, radiating outward. Each of us is a battery—a resonator, generating waves of electromagnetic energy.

Sacred drumming strengthens and harmonizes the electromagnetic fields of our bodies and projects this harmony into all realms of existence. The drum attunes us and our environment. Through sacred drumming, the masculine/feminine currents within the individual resonate in harmony with those of the Earth. The creative currents that flow within the human body, flow across the surface of the planet.

According to the Hopi creation myth, it was Tiowa, the Creator, who created the Earth. The Earth, however, was void of life, so Tiowa created Spider Woman. Spider Woman descended from heaven to Earth on a spiral web. She took some soil, mixed it with saliva, and molded it into two beings. She sang the "Creation Song", bringing the twins to life. She named one twin Poqanghoya and sent him to the North Pole to create the structures and forms of life. She named the other twin Palonghoya and sent him to the South Pole to sound out the voice of Tiowa, the heartbeat throbbing at the center of the universe.

Reaching the southern pole, Palonghoya began beating his drum, linking himself in harmony with the Creator. As he drummed, life-force energy flowed into the navel of the Earth at the South Pole and resounded along the Earth's axis from pole to pole. Life-force energy coursed down into the crystal core of the planet. From the activated core, currents of life-force energy radiated outward through the crust, bringing the entire planet to life. From the North Pole, Paqanghoya structured the life-force into a web around the planet.

An etheric web of sacred energy meridians envelops Earth. This electromagnetic grid is largely the result of interaction between the magnetic field, emanating from the planet's molten iron-nickel core dynamo, and the electrically charged gas of the ionosphere.[1] The masculine/electrical meridians tend to flow in the high mountains and the feminine/magnetic meridians generally flow through the low lying hills, valleys, and bodies of water. The lines and intersection points of this energy grid match most of Earth's seismic fracture zones and ocean ridges, as well as worldwide atmospheric highs and lows, paths of migratory birds, gravitational anomalies, and the sites of ancient temples and megalithic structures.[2]

Early man discovered these planetary currents called ley lines. In China they were known as Dragon Currents. The Aborigines of Australia know them as a "line of songs". In England, the Druids referred to the Old Straight Track. Native Americans regarded the energy pattern as the Serpent Power or the Great Dragons. According to Cherokee tradition, the dragons once followed the will of the great shamans who would invoke them to protect the people and the land.

Through a type of dowsing called geomancy, the ley lines were located and marked. Roads or pathways were often constructed along the ley lines, such as those leading out of Chaco Canyon, New Mexico, or the series of tracks emanating from Cuzco, Peru, the ancient Incan capital. In China, Dragon Currents marked all sacred paths and centers throughout the country. Visible lines tie together every major religious site in England. Early Christian churches were located along the currents, their steeples acting to unite heaven and earthly energies.

The early geomancers discovered that the numinous planetary grid is the equivalent to the acupuncture meridian system of the human body. Humans, they perceived, were created in the image of Mother Earth. The acupuncture and node points of the human body correspond to those of Earth's.

At the intersection points of the planet's energy ley lines exist holy places, power spots, or acupuncture points. Primal peoples interacted geomantically with grid nodes by building such landscape temples as Stonehenge and the Great Pyramid. They performed sacred rituals and ceremonies within the temples to harmonize the descending heavenly energies with Earth's terrestrial energies, thereby uniting heaven and Earth.

The sacred rituals of the Native Americans and other primal peoples around the world served to maintain the harmonious flow of the planetary energy currents. As part of the Creator's plan, each tribe or clan was assigned a particular region to care for. The Cherokee, for example, were originally instructed to serve as caretakers of the Smokey Mountains. The Cherokee (like all primal peoples) understood that the land did not belong to them, but instead they belonged in this particular region. They performed their sacred ceremonies and rituals to maintain a harmonious balance of the energy currents of the entire planet. They thought globally, but acted locally.

The Hopi clans, upon their emergence into the Fourth World, were each instructed to make four directional migrations across the continent before they all arrived at their common permanent home. The migrations were purification ceremonies that lasted for hundreds of years. The clans left behind monuments of their passage—the great ruins of stone pueblos and cliff dwellings. All their routes formed a great cross whose center lay in what is now the Hopi reservation of Arizona. At the center of the cross formed by their migrations lay the "Center of the Universe". "It is not the geographic center of North America, but the magnetic or spiritual center formed by the junction of the north-south and the east-west axes along which the Creator sends vibratory messages and controls the rotation of the planet."[3] The Hopi know that they were led to this harsh and arid region so that they would have to depend upon and preserve their sacred rituals and ceremonies in order to evoke the necessary rainfall to survive. Here they strive to consolidate the universal plan of creation and maintain the harmony of the planet.

The Maya of the Yucatan and Central America left behind a sophisticated science of geomancy in their hieroglyphic inscriptions that adorn their temples and stepped pyramids. The Mayan ley system was part of an intergalactic network of energy forms. It incorporated three levels of environment: the upper level of constellations and planets, the middle level of the Earth's surface, and the lower level of underground streams and mineral deposits. The Maya developed a sacred calendar, the Tzolkin, to track the cyclical harmonics of the planetary grid. "They used their harmonic science to harmonize and distribute the energy of the grid in accordance with daily, weekly, monthly, seasonal, and yearly cycles."[4]

"Black Mesa of the Hopi plateau, the Black Hills, and other areas are pathways of lunar (feminine) energy. The Tibetan Plateau, the Rainbow Serpent Mountains of Australia, and others are focal points of solar (masculine) energy."[5] The Great Pyramid, Stonehenge, Mt. Shasta, California, Machu Picchu, Peru, Easter Island, and the North and South Poles are all nodal points where masculine and feminine energies converge. Secondary grid energy lines branch out like the spokes of a wheel from these primary node points and interconnect to form secondary power spots. The pattern continues to branch out, forming a complex web that links together all life forms.

The continuous pulsation of the grid slowly, but inevitably shapes the infrastructure of the planet. It forms and maintains the biosphere, shields the Earth from cosmic radiation, functions as a geologic regulator, and emanates the basic pulse of the Creator that guides the evolution of the planet. Gaia's etheric body remains sentiently active, a model or blueprint of "paradise".

The ancient myths of virtually all Earth peoples speak of a time of harmony and balance—of paradise. This planet may not have always been like it is now with dramatic climate swings, earthquakes, pole wobble, and the like. Reshaped and warped by tectonic plate activity, artificial electromagnetic pollution, and massive nuclear testing, the planetary grid is out of alignment. Modern day dowsers, shamans, and medicine people are tracking the new grid and working to activate and harmonize its currents.

Earth and humans exist in a reciprocal bioresonant relationship. Through the Earth's resonant gridwork, we affect our environment and our environment in turn affects us. By interphasing with Earth's sacred places, we are capable of generating a world of peace and harmony. Seek out power places. Your power spots can be identified by your desire to go to them. Their significance to you is always revealed by your planned or accidental presence at them. You will respond more quickly and naturally to a geographical location that is the same type as your own energy, be it electric, magnetic, or electromagnetic. In time you may develop the sensitivity necessary to feel the energies of the planet. You may sense a subtle tingling in your hands or feet when near a power spot.

Mountains, rivers, and waterfalls are powerful places to drum. Mountainous regions charge you with energy and counteract imbalances or negativity. Mountains are generally electrical and projective in nature, emanating great spiritual power. Sacred mountains are places of access to the divine power of all creation, or as openings to higher intuitive consciousness. They are excellent places to drum for planetary healing.

Rivers, lakes, and other bodies of water are magnetic/receptive in nature. Being near a body of water is very beneficial. It is soothing and relaxing. Magnetic fields influence the pineal gland or third eye, and heighten the subconscious. Bodies of water help to expand and clarify the inner vision and are conducive to stimulating the flow of creative and healing energies, and sharpening telepathic abilities. A close proximity to water helps cleanse the mind and body. Rivers, in particular, are good places for planetary healing, for the healing energy generated will flow and spread downstream. Water is a profound conductor of energy.

Waterfalls are electromagnetic in nature. The water itself is magnetic. Electric energy is produced by the falling water.

The two forces combine to form electromagnetic energy. Such energy is of a balanced, harmonic nature. It is a powerful, creative, synthesizing energy that helps to balance the masculine/feminine aspects of nature.

Great healing can be accomplished by physically going to sacred power spots or by placing your focus and intent upon such places from a distance. The energy of power sites is greatest during equinoxes, solstices, and full moons. These areas are highly sensitive to sacred drumming as impetus to harmonizing the descending divine energy against the chaos of negative individual, national, and planetary thought patterns. Negative or discordant energy can be transmuted by creating positive energy and thoughts. The masculine and feminine forces are then balanced and amplified, distributing great harmony throughout the planetary grid.

Heal Mother Earth by drumming the celestial side of the drum with your intent and prayers focused upon healing the planet. Pray that your negative thought patterns and those of others be transmuted and balanced. When you switch to the lowerworld side of the drum, focus your attention inward to the base of the spine. When you focus upon your root chakra, you are also focused upon the root chakra of the planet. The descending divine energy of harmony will thus be grounded within you and into the Earth upon which you sit. End with a round of drumming on the celestial side, offering thanks.

Practice drumming celestial bodies as outlined in Chapter Four on Power Practice. In this manner, you become a direct conduit of the vast source energy emanating from the stars. By drumming celestial bodies on a sacred power spot or ley line, this healing energy is amplified even more and channeled directly into Earth's etheric web.

Healing energy can also be directed to negative or problem areas around the world, such as fault lines, oil spills, nuclear test sites, and war torn countries. To practice distant Earth healing, form your intent and drum the celestial side of the drum. You could pray that the divine energy be allowed to merge with the basic elements of Earth, Water, Fire, and Air to eliminate all imbalance within the problem area. When you shift to the lowerworld side of the drum, place your focus upon the area in need so that the source energy you are drawing upon will be directed there.

Keepers of the Earth

It is important to heal Earth now, for the time of "Purification" or "Cleansing" will soon come. The Earth may cleanse herself in cataclysmic fashion as she has done before. How destructive the cleansing will be depends upon how many humans change their attitudes toward the planet and begin treating her with love and respect, and live a life of harmony with all that exists.

Earth changes occur when imbalances need to be corrected. As a species, we have created a great deal of negative energy which now inundates the ionosphere. The ionosphere is that electrically charged atmosphere that exists outside the stratosphere and extends several hundred miles out into space. It forms a protective barrier around the planet. Negativity, in the form of individual thought patterns multiplied many millions of times, is capable of creating a physical imbalance and depleting the ionosphere. The negative thought patterns of every individual who ever existed continue to exist in the Earth's framework until transmuted. (The auric field of the human body is also a storehouse of negative thought patterns.) The ionosphere needs to have its mass rebuilt through sufficient positive energy and a change in general awareness of humanity, for its depletion will result in Earth's demise.

In addition, we are today awash in a sea of energies life has never before experienced. For billions of years, the energies that life flourished within were relatively simple. There was a subtle electromagnetic grid surrounding the planet and a few weak radio waves which reached the Earth from the sun and other stars. Light was the most abundant form of electromagnetic energy. We will never experience that quiet world again. The human species has altered the electromagnetic field more than any other aspect of the environment. "The density of radio waves around us is now 100 million to 200 million times the natural level reaching us from the sun."[6] Radar, television, radio, microwaves, and high tension power lines all contaminate the planet's natural field.

All living things share in the common experience of being plugged into the electromagnetic fields of the planet. All life pulsates in time to Earth's extremely low frequencies which are concentrated at about ten hertz (cycles per second). This alpha rhythm is the primary frequency in all animals. Artificial fields cause abnormal reactions in all organisms. Electropollution creates stronger diseases and weakens immune systems. The biological systems of all living things are impaired. The natural frequencies of the planet's electromagnetic web are drowned out. We literally can't hear the voice of Mother Earth anymore.

We must attune ourselves again to the planet and the alpha frequency is the key. We must replace discordant thoughts, actions, and deeds with harmonious ones. We must transmute the negative dissonant energy that we have created over the course of human history. We must solve the environmental and social problems that beset this planet. We must effect these positive changes, each one of us.

We find ourselves in a predicament, another lesson we must learn before we can ascend to higher realms. The reality we have co-created over the course of written history has served a purpose, which was to bring about in humanity an evolution. As our awareness expands in this information age, we become conscious of our role as custodians of this garden, "Gaia". The forces of nature await our guidance.

This hugh, spinning, elliptical gyroscope revolving around the sun is a dynamo of energy. It generates and channels the primary forces that formed this evolving universe. The very forces that pulse through and around us. We channel these forces without being aware of it. These energies have great power to destroy as we can see by the current state of affairs in our world. They also have much greater power to create, to create new realities, a new world—paradise. We must learn to channel these forces in a positive mode of good will. As we attune to these forces, our awareness expands and we ascend to higher levels of consciousness, harmonizing with the upper realms of ecstasy. Ecstasy and paradise await us as we relearn the sacred knowledge that floats in waves all around us—electromagnetic waves that vibrate throughout the universe.

Nature is conscious of its role in the evolution of this planet. Only man exists on this green planet, stumbling along in unconsciousness. We are composed of the very forces that create and direct the evolution of the universe. We are composed of diverging waves of energy, compressed and manifested into physical form by the weight of gravity and the binding nature of atoms.

Modern physics has transported humanity into a new awareness. These astounding discoveries only affirm the great mysteries left to be discovered and experienced. A great mysterious plan affects our evolution as a species. The mystery is what we are here to experience. Other dimensions of reality await our discovery. As we alter our states of consciousness, we attune ourselves to the forces of nature and begin to channel them through divine guidance.

The age we live in is one we all chose. Whatever our path, it's one we have freely chosen. Whatever our reality, it is one we have created. However, we are not living this present lifetime for ourselves. We are here to serve. We have a debt to repay. We have created a great deal of negative energy upon this planet. We have upset the balance of the planetary ecosystem. The ancient prophecies of many primal peoples warn us that Earth will cleanse herself in cataclysmic fashion as she has done before, unless humanity listens once again to her subtle voice. Any prophecy, however, can be altered by a change in consciousness, or at least eased somewhat.

Shamanic drumming is one way we can heal and harmonize the energies of this planet. However, the ancient drumming ways will be of little use to you unless you yourself respect all forms of life and seek harmony in your life and environment. It is human consciousness that must first change. It is easier to cleanse toxins from the planet than to remove the toxic thoughts that cause them from human minds. We are all one. Everything is interconnected by waves of energy for the universe is a web of inseparable energy patterns. In time you may see threads, grids, and webs of light upon your journeys. Work the drum to heal these webs of energy. The more you drum, the more you empower, heal, and harmonize the energy patterns of yourself, the planet, and the universe. Through drumming alone, we can renew the wave of harmony because the drum's sonorous voice carries the energy of transformation. We manifest the "Sacred Vision".

DREAMING THE DRUM

Drums are a dream arisen,
Weaving the tapestry of life.
Drums bear seekers of vision,
Embracing the rainbow of light.

Cherokee

Afterword

Healing involves body, mind, and spirit. The shaman recognizes this unity and treats all three, but most importantly, the shaman must offer enlightenment—must help the patient understand his or her place in the universe. Healing is of little value if the patient continues to live in disharmony. The symptoms will only return. The shaman helps the patient discover a power within him or herself that is greater than the power that produced the symptom. The shaman heals people by taking them out of themselves, by altering their consciousness, by sharing the ecstasy.

An adept shaman theoretically needs only well developed powers of intuition and imagination to perform a healing. Incantations, ceremonies, and rituals are cultural symbols of the healing state that the shaman incorporates for the benefit of the sick patient. Healing is a powerful, culturally entrenched ritual. Healing is better achieved when the shaman and patient share the same cultural myths. The shaman is much more effective in influencing others when operating within their perceptions of reality. The world today needs shamans who can function within the cultural contexts of modern societies.

The pursuit of Amerindian cultural ceremonials and rituals serves little purpose for the non-indian. Each of us should develop ceremonies based upon our own vision and intuition. We are drawn to Native American teachings because they are so pure and harmonious, and because the planet is calling out, trying to reach each and every one of us. We must each find our own path by sitting down and listening to what the Earth Mother asks of us. The voice of the Earth is a pulse within us and drumming aligns us with that pulse. When your heartbeat is one with Earth's, you may begin to feel, look, and act much like traditional Native Americans, for they too resonate with her.

What is your deepest inner longing? What is it you wish to do more than anything else? Whatever it is, it will carry you to what you need to do next in order to manifest your life's purpose, even if you don't yet know what that purpose is. When something is easily presented to you, and it sounds like a wonderful and enjoyable thing to do, then by all means do it. That is guidance. Break down the barriers that society has imprisoned you with. Let yourself flow with the energy dance of the ceremony of life. If you don't, you block guidance and halt your growth.

True security only comes with a clear understanding of your place and role in the universe. To achieve such a level is often a life-long, on going process. Shamanic drumming can aid us in this process of growth and evolvement. The drum will always find a pathway for those who have proper intent (help or healing), clarity of mind (clear of doubt), and purity of heart. Wallace Black Elk, the renowned Lakota shaman, speaks of this spiritual power: "When you pray with that drum, when the spirits hear that drum, it echoes. They hear this drum, and they hear your voice loud and clear."[1] The drum amplifies and carries our prayers and intent into all realms of existence. Its rhythm is a universal language.

The drum functions as an instrument of attunement. The drum's rhythm synchronizes the left and right hemispheres of the brain, stimulates a holistic alpha brain wave cycle, renews the flow of the intuitive mind, harmonizes the spiritual and physical aspects of one's being, and links the consciousness of one being to another, uniting the universe and its diverse life forms completely.

When we practice sacred drumming, we become one with what we are made of. We become one with the voice of the Great Spirit, that primal rhythm that pulses within all that exists. We transcend time and space and soar on flights of rapture and ecstasy. We pierce the veil of illusion into the radiance of the "Sacred Vision".

Acquiring Drums

Traditional medicine or shamanic drums are hand-drums. They are smaller, light drums which can easily be held in one hand, leaving the other hand free to beat the drum. They are narrow drums in which the hide is stretched over a frame or hoop three inches or less in width and may vary from eight to twenty-four inches in diameter. They may be single-headed or double-headed. Like all rawhide drums, they do not have a fixed pitch. Heating and cooling the hide raises and lowers the pitch, but a specific tone cannot be maintained.

Acquiring a suitable shamanic drum is often difficult since we no longer live in a primitive tribal society. The craft of drummaking is disappearing, even among traditional native peoples. If they can be found, two-headed rawhide drums are far superior because of their balance, varying pitches, and harmonic overtones. One side of the drum produces the rhythmic beating tone while the other side sings and hums. The finest authentic two-headed rawhide drums are made by the Taos Indians of New Mexico. Taos drums can easily be found in Taos and Santa Fe, New Mexico. They may also be obtained from: The Taos Drum Company, P.O. Box 1916, Taos, New Mexico 87571; (505) 758-3796. Another fine drummaker is Rodney Scott, 3555 Singing Pines Road, Dept. WF, Darby MT 59829; (406) 821-4401.

Outside the southwestern United States, rawhide drums are very difficult, if not impossible to obtain. Do not hesitate, however, to try out any drum you may already have or can borrow, or even buy. Conga drums, Latin bongos, Celtic drums, and even snare drums (remove the snare) are possibilities. You might also consider the "REMO Pre-tuned Hand Drum". It is an inexpensive single-headed round frame drum with a mylar head. It can be obtained in most musical instrument stores or by writing: Boston Music Co., 116 Boylston Street, Boston, MA 02116; (617) 426-5100. You will have to experiment with different kinds of drumsticks since the hand does not produce the necessary sharpness of sound. You might try standard wooden drumsticks, or slightly padded sticks.

Another possibility is to make your own rawhide drum. Crafting and playing a drum that you have made yourself is eminently more satisfying than playing any other. A drum of your own creation will be imbued with your own unique essence. It will become a powerful extension of yourself. To guide you in drummaking, I highly recommend the paperback book, *How To Make Drums, Tomtoms, and Rattles; Primitive Percussion Instruments for Modern Use* by Bernard S. Mason, published by Dover Publications, Inc., 180 Varick Street, New York, NY 10014. Originally published in 1938, this unabridged republication is a storehouse of information on the craft of drummaking. Securing the necessary rawhide may prove to be the most difficult part of crafting your own drum. Untanned deer and elk hides are the most suitable and authentic. Rawhide may be obtained by contacting local tanneries, taxidermists, and glove manufacturers. Rawhide and drummaking materials may also be obtained from: Akers Drums, 1303 Astor Street, Bellingham, WA 98225; (206) 734-1085.

Cassette recordings of shamanic drumming can be purchased at many record and tape outlets and metaphysical bookstores. When used with a high quality stereo with optimal bass response, a sympathetic resonance between the drums and the body/consciousness is provided. The effects are similar to those of having a real drum in the room. The healing vibrations of the recording may lack the intensity of the actual drum, yet such tapes allow complete freedom to journey without the necessity of placing part of the conscious mind on the physical aspects of beating the drum. It takes time and practice to relax and allow the intuitive mind to flow, while at the same time maintaining a regular drum beat.

Cassettes and portable cassette players with headphones allow you to alter your consciousness anywhere and anytime without disturbing others, or when using a drum may be impractical. However, one should avoid listening to shamanic drumming tapes while driving a vehicle or operating heavy machinery. There are times when entering altered states is inappropriate, so use discretion. More information on acquiring shamanic drumming cassettes and drums may be obtained by writing: The Foundation For Shamanic Studies, PO Box 670, Belden Station, Norwalk, Connecticut 06852. Another source of information and drumming cassettes is Brooke Medicine Eagle, Sky Lodge, PO Box 121-5D, Ovando, MT 59854.

Chakras

Chakra is a Sanskrit word meaning "wheel" and is a circular energy center through which life-force travels. There are seven major chakras arranged linearly along the vertical spinal axis from the scrotum to the crown of the head. There are from seven to twenty-two minor chakras in the human body. The seven primary chakras are like electrical junction boxes for the physical body, mediating life-force energy throughout the human body. They are the interface between the physical and the spiritual aspects of one's being.

The Seven Major Chakras

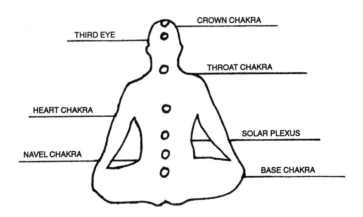

The seventh and highest chakra spins at the crown (center/top) of the head. It is the open door through which divine communication is received. It is associated with the color violet and the musical note B. Its energy reflects personal identification with the Infinite—with the great spiritual issues of life.

The sixth chakra is that of the brow or "third eye". It is the seat of spiritual intuition and inner vision. It is connected to the pineal gland. It is associated with the color indigo and the musical note A. It is located between and slightly above the eyebrows.

The fifth chakra is known as the throat chakra and is connected to the thyroid gland. It expresses one's ability to communicate or express "truth" through power of the spoken word. Its musical note is G and its color is blue. It is located at the base of the neck in the nook where the clavicle bones meet.

The fourth chakra is the heart chakra and is naturally connected to the heart as well as the thymus gland. The heart chakra is the balancing point of heavenly and earthly energies. It balances the descending higher chakra energies against the ascending lower chakra frequencies. It expresses soul/heart consciousness and love. It is located at the center of the chest in direct line with the nipples. Its color is green and musical note is F.

The third chakra is in the area of the solar plexus and is connected to the spleen. Its energy expresses personal power. It is the area where personal power is stored. This is an important chakra, for the accumulation and maintenance of power are fundamental to shamanic practice. Its color is yellow and musical note is E. It is located beneath the ribs directly below the sternum.

The second chakra is the navel chakra. It is the chakra of sexuality and emotion, and is located in the region of the reproductive organs. It functions in the utilization of creative forces into all aspects of one's being. This chakra is located slightly below the navel. Its color is orange and musical note D.

The first chakra or root chakra is located at the base of the spine. It functions in grounding the spiritual forces in the body to the Earth and the physical realm of reality. It reflects one's ability to function effectively on a day-to-day basis. When poorly grounded, your spatial understanding is impaired. You may stumble around both physically and mentally as well as emotionally. The root chakra is connected to the adrenals. Its color is red and musical note middle C.

There are symbolic power animals associated with each of the seven chakras. In many shamanic cultures, when a shaman acquires a new power animal, the energy center associated with that animal becomes active. Some cultures consider it dangerous to open an energy center without first acquiring the wisdom of the power animal related to that specific chakra. The power animals associated with individual chakras vary from culture to culture. However, the highest chakra is generally considered the perch of Eagle, while Horse is tethered to the lowest chakra.

According to the sacred teachings of the Hopi, Cherokee, Tibetan, and Hindu peoples, the living body of man and the living body of Earth were created in the perfect image of the Creator. Through both man and Earth run an axis. Man's axis is the backbone which controls the equilibrium of his movements. The axis of the Earth runs from the north to the south pole and controls the rotation and orbit of the planet. "There are seven vibratory centers along man's backbone and seven along the earth's axis and they all echo the call of the Creator."[1]

At each stage of man's evolution one of these psychophysical centers functions in a predominant way. For each stage of man's mind/body evolution there is created a corresponding development in the Earth. Each successive period of development concludes with catastrophic destruction to both Earth and mankind due to humanity's fall from grace. Each world stage was destroyed because humans misused their vibratory centers for selfish purposes and forgot their spiritual roles in the Creator's evolutionary plan. Ascending upward, each new stage unfolds at a higher level of mind/body awareness. There have been three previous worlds before this present one. This fourth cycle is ending as we enter yet another realm—a higher octave of consciousness.

The seven chakras are also linked to the seven branched "World Tree". The "Tree of Life" and the major chakras both represent the seven stages of man's evolution, as well as the conduit of the Creator's life-force and divine wisdom. The spinal column enables us to be rooted in the Earth. This axis of transformation is often symbolized by the ascent of the coiled (Quetzalcoatl) serpent. The nervous system is the gateway to heaven.

Through the energy centers of our bodies we are in communion with the Earth, stars, and all creation. The energies of creation are coming together within us all the time. We must attune ourselves again to these rhythms and cycles through which we are interacting with the entire universe. We must become attuned to the change in rhythm taking place in this new cycle. In doing so, we synchronize ourselves and our environment to the larger cycle of the sacred wheel—the cycle of all that exists.

The voice of creation sings its song within us. Each chakra is like a note on the musical scale. As the notes played on an instrument sound overtones that generate multiple harmonies, so too do the human chakras generate fields of great harmonic resonance. Every human has an obligation to share with the planet and "all our relations" the vibrations of harmony.

The drum is a powerful instrument of attunement. The vibrations of the drum remove blockages in chakras that may impede the flow of higher energy. By focusing inward upon the individual chakras, we cleanse and empower them (while drumming), we explore and learn from them. By focusing upon the third eye, we stimulate inner vision. By focusing upon the solar plexus, we learn about power. By focusing upon the root chakra, we learn how to work lovingly on the physical plane, and how to ground the spiritual into the physical.

There is a perfect pattern encoded in the vibrations of our chakras. To resonate more and more with this pattern creates transformation. Through repeated drummings the chakra system becomes sensitive and attuned to harmonic resonance. This field of harmonic resonance spirals out, interacting with all that exists.

Medicine Wheel of Life

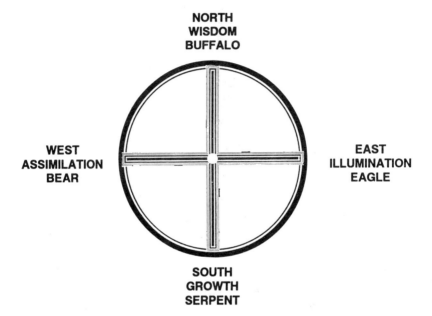

NORTH
WISDOM
BUFFALO

WEST
ASSIMILATION
BEAR

EAST
ILLUMINATION
EAGLE

SOUTH
GROWTH
SERPENT

Within the cosmology of primal peoples, the circle represents life. All aspects of life, energy, and the ever-moving universe spiral in circles. The plants, the animals, the minerals, and the elemental forces of nature all exist within the circle. All creatures walk the circumference of the Medicine Wheel Of Life, experiencing birth, life, and death. After completing a cycle of learning on the sacred wheel, each of us returns to the Source, the Great Mystery at the center of the circle.

The Medicine Wheel Of Life is symbolized by a circle which is bisected first with a line of light from East to West. From the East the sun arises and the guardian Eagle takes flight. The energy of the East is the power of illumination, inspiration, and ascending consciousness.

From the South rises the vital energy of renewal, regeneration, and growth. From the South we learn to plant seeds of good cause. We learn that our thoughts and actions create our reality. The Serpent is regarded as the guardian of the South.

From the West flows the energy of transformation. The guardian animal of the West is the Bear. In the West we assimilate our life experiences. Experience is the only baggage we carry with us from this Earth walk. From the West we exit the realm of physical experience and join into vast levels of experience in the spirit worlds of light, or we choose to return and walk again the sacred wheel of life.

From the North flows the energy that completes the quartering of the circle. From the North we receive wisdom and clarity of mind. The totemic guardian of the North is the Buffalo.

Quartering the circle defines all that is the Great Mystery. We are here on Earth to experience and realize the Mystery. The vision of that mystery is ever present within each of us. When we still the incessant chatter of the mind, we begin to realize the Sacred Vision. We begin to recognize certain qualities from the four directions that help us spiral toward completion, toward harmony and balance.

Father Sky and Mother Earth together generate the powers of creation. The four directions are the power and life-giving forces of the created. When we begin in the East and turn clockwise, acknowledging the four directions, we align ourselves with the powers that shape our reality. We acknowledge that we are each co-creators of the evolving universe. The energies of creation are coming together within us all the time. These creative energies spiral in rhythms and cycles that ebb and flow. Sacred drumming attunes us to these rhythms and cycles, and synchronizes us and our environment to the larger cycle of the sacred wheel, the cycle of all that exists.

The Single-headed Drum

The cosmology and methodology presented in this book represent the shamanic drum ways I learned which incorporate the use of a two-headed drum. A single-headed drum, however, can be used just as effectively in shamanic work. Though the drum varies from culture to culture in its size, shape, and construction, its spiritual power is universal.

The single-headed drum is more prevalent among Native American tribes of the Western Plains such as the Lakota and Blackfeet, as well as Northwest Coastal and Alaskan tribes. As with all arts and crafts, the cosmology of these tribes is often depicted on the single-headed drum with symbolic designs. The entire world or universe may be painted on the outside of the drumhead. The upper half of the drumhead might be painted white or red to represent the sky world, while the lower half could be colored green or black to symbolize the underworld. Other drums are often painted with a medicine wheel design which represents the ever-spiraling universe (See Appendix C, Medicine Wheel Of Life). Such symbolism infuses the single-headed drum with the powers of creation. The single-headed drum, like the double-headed drum, represents a microcosm of the universe.

If you are using a single-headed drum for shamanic drumming, you could beat the upper half of the drumhead while drumming the celestial realm, and then drum the lower half for the underworld (See Chapter 3, The Fundamentals of Shamanic Drumming). However, even this is unnecessary if your intent is focused. You could merely focus your intent, prayers, and consciousness on the sky or celestial realm during the first round of drumming. On the second round of drumming, place your focus on the underworld, then end with a final round of celestial focus. Intent is the power that shapes our reality. So whether your drum is single or double-headed, it is the focus of your intent and the life-force generated by drumming that renew the sacred hoop of harmony and balance.

Journeys

This appendix describes several shamanic journeys that I have undertaken while drumming. They were vivid and powerful experiences for me. Though your own experiences will be unique, you may be interested in comparing your journeys with these.

1. The drumbeats carried me away on the wings of an eagle. I soared high over South Sister (a volcanic peak in the Cascade Range), then dove into a cave on her south flank. Clear quartz crystals shimmered from the walls, floor, and ceiling. I transformed into a man and followed a narrow path through the crystal cave. The path led me through a maze of twists and turns until the cave ended in a wall of crystals. A small hole appeared in the wall and sucked me or my awareness into a dark tunnel. I spiraled downward and came out of the tunnel onto the rim of a red mesa. I saw a pueblo below me at the base of the mesa. I heard drumming and chanting and saw many dancers.

Suddenly, I became one of the dancers. I gazed at the Pueblo Indian beating the drum. He wore a red bandanna around the crown of his head. He smiled at me and chanted loudly. At the sound of his chant, I transformed into a golden eagle and took flight. I circled the pueblo, then glided over the desert. I soared towards the sun high above the Earth. I saw the Earth below change into a beautiful clear crystal. The sun spoke to me and asked me my totem. "I am the Eagle and the Wolf," I said. "I stalk power and power stalks me."

I then flew back to the Earth and across the desert to a cliff dwelling built high in the alcove of a limestone cliff. I flew into a doorway or window and transformed once again into a man. I looked at the floor of the room and saw the white bones of a skeleton. The skeleton arose, transforming into a beautiful Indian woman. She walked toward me and gently caressed my cheek with her hand. She smiled and said, "I am your wife and guide." I clasped her outstretched hand and we both transformed into golden eagles and flew away from the cliff dwelling. We soared the blue sky above the desert. As the sun began to set on the horizon, we separated and I returned rapidly to the red mesa above the pueblo. I entered a small hole in the top of the mesa and retraced the passage back to my body.

The preceding journey was one of the first I had ever undertaken. The spirit guide I encountered was once my wife in a previous life, and she has since guided me on many journeys. Her name is Corn Woman and her medicine power is great. One year after undertaking this journey, I met the drummer that I had encountered in the vision. The shaman's name is Jade Wah'oo and when I met him in Arizona he was wearing a red bandanna and beating a drum.

2. The drumbeats carried me away to the crystal cave on the south face of South Sister. I entered the cave and the quartz crystals glowed with the colors of the rainbow. A rainbow of crystals spiraled out before me through the passageway. I absorbed their energy and was swept through the cave to the wall of crystals at the end of the cave. I was sucked through the hole in the wall and a rainbow of light trailed behind me.

I came out of the tunnel atop the red mesa and sat down to look at a beautiful rainbow that arched the sky above the pueblo below me. It had just rained and the clear air was scented with the aroma of sage. All was quiet at the pueblo below. It seemed deserted, but then I heard and saw the drummer in a plaza below. Suddenly, I was sitting opposite him. I closed my eyes, and when I opened them, he was gone. The drum, however, continued to beat. Rattlesnakes began to appear all around me, but I was not afraid. I became a huge snake and coiled at the center of the ring of snakes. I then crawled down into a burrow and went deep into the Earth. It was dark, and when I finally came out of the burrow I was underwater. My awareness merged with the ocean of blue water. I felt the liquid ebb and flow of the water through and around me. I sensed the female energy. I felt the moon pulling at me, pulling at the tides.

I finally arose from the sea as an eagle and soared towards the sun. I waited for it to speak, but the sun said nothing, so I returned to Earth and flew across the desert to Montezuma's Castle (a cliff dwelling in central Arizona). I called out to Corn Woman to guide me. She stared out at me through a window, then came out into the plaza to greet me. We embraced and I felt warm and safe in her presence. She told me that we must wait for power.

We sat down before the cliff dwelling and it began to rain. A dark thunderstorm approached and lightning bolts struck all around us. Thunder rolled and boomed, shaking the ground beneath us. Out of the storm came a man, an Indian. He approached us and sat down opposite me. Corn Woman sat to one side and beat a drum. The rain beat down around us, soaking our hair and clothing. The man held out his hand and I grasped it. Power surged through me, the power of thunder and lightning. We raised both of our arms and our hands met, palm to palm.

The Earth cracked between us and swallowed us. We fell into the dark depths and my vision became muddled and confused. I called out to Corn Woman to guide me, for I felt lost and disoriented. She came to me and embraced me and I felt safe in the haven of her arms. The darkness receded and she told me that the journey was almost over. She said that my power was waning and that is why my journey became disoriented. She told me to return and so I did.

The preceding journey put me in touch with my own feminine energy. The man who emerged from the storm appeared to me several days later as a guide and teacher in the material world. Another synchronicity occurred only minutes after the journey ended when the sound of thunder boomed overhead. The thunderstorm resounded throughout the afternoon.

I undertook the following journey to acquire the power animal of a friend. It is a good illustration of what one may encounter on such a journey. The power animal that I was seeking revealed itself in a very powerful way. For the sake of brevity, only the initial part of the journey is presented.

3. I soared on the wings of an eagle to Montezuma's Castle and flew into a window. I went spiraling down through a ribbed tunnel. It became narrower and narrower until my body slipped along the smooth walls of a birth canal. Far below I saw a light. I slid toward the light and emerged from the birth canal. I uncoiled from the fetal position and stood in the bright light. I looked up at a yellow/orange sun. I spoke to the sun, telling it that I was searching for the power animal of Kathy. The sun smiled upon me and a cloud floated overhead. From out of the cloud came a bolt of lightning that struck the ground before me. It created a hole in the ground and from out of the hole came a badger.

"Badger," I said. "You are one of my power animals. Can you tell me the guardian animal of my friend Kathy?"

"Look skyward," it said.

I looked up and saw a bird swooping down from the sun. It was a red-tailed hawk. I held out my arm and the hawk perched on my wrist. "Tell me red-tailed hawk," I said. "What is the power animal of my friend?"

The hawk took wing into the blue sky, I took wing as the Eagle and followed it. We soared across a red desert and came to a stream or creek. I descended to a deer beside the stream. I asked the deer of Kathy's power animal. The deer bounded away and I followed it through a vast field of tall grass. The autumn grass was parched and brown and rose above my head. I saw a huge buffalo standing in the tall grass to my right and another one to my left. I continued to follow the deer until I lost sight of it. I gazed up into the deep blue sky. I fell back into the grass upon my back and gazed aimlessly into Father Sky. A flock of geese flew overhead in a V-formation. A coyote emerged from the grass and licked me playfully on the face.

"Tell me coyote," I said. "Do you know the power animal of Kathy?"

The coyote howled and sang a beautiful song to the sun. It then told me to look skyward. I looked up and there was the red-tailed hawk, powerful, majestic, swooping down over my head. I turned to watch the hawk and found Corn Woman standing before me. Her long black hair and brown eyes were a welcome sight. I looked into her eyes and smiled. "Corn Woman, I have come seeking the power animal of a woman warrior."

"Yes, I see her," she said. "Her spirit is with us now."

I turned and saw Kathy standing behind me. My heart soared. The three of us sat down upon the ground, forming a triangle with me at the apex. We joined hands and called upon the powers of the sky, the Earth, and the four directions. We called out for Kathy's power animal to come forth. We heard the rumble as the ground shook beneath us. Four buffalo came forth. They circled us and stood at the four cardinal points.

Not every journey one undertakes will necessarily be coherent, vivid, or powerful. Still, no matter how esoteric or random the experience may seem, it adds to one's shamanic power and knowledge. Seemingly insignificant events in a journey or vision may manifest in a powerful way in your ordinary state of awareness. Be on the lookout for these powerful synchronicities, for they confirm that your shamanic work is producing positive effects.

Notes

Introduction

1. Harner, Michael. *The Way of the Shaman.* New York: Harper and Row, 1980.

Chapter 1: The Role of the Drum

1. Eliade, Mircea. *Shamanism: Archaic Techniques of Ecstasy.* Princeton: Princeton University Press, 1972.
2. Ywahoo, Dhyani. *Voices of Our Ancestors: Cherokee Teachings From the Wisdom Fire.* Boston: Shambhala, 1987.
3. Ywahoo, Dhyani. *Voices of Our Ancestors: Cherokee Teachings From the Wisdom Fire.* Boston: Shambhala, 1987.
4. Corballis, Michael C., and Beale, Ivan L. *The Ambivalent Mind.* Chicago: Nelson-Hall, 1983.
5. Neher, Andrew. "A Psychological Explanation of Unusual Behavior in Ceremonies Involving Drums". *Human Biology,* 34(2), 1962: pp. 151-160.
6. Harner, Michael. *The Way of the Shaman.* New York: Harper and Row, 1980.
7. Elkin, A.P. *Aboriginal Men of High Degree.* Second Edition. New York: St. Martin's Press, 1977.

Chapter 2: The Cosmology of the Drum

1. Campbell, Joseph. *The Flight of the Wild Gander.* South Bend: Regnery/Gateway, Inc., 1979.
2. Brown, Joseph Epes. *The Sacred Pipe: Black Elk's Account of the Seven Rites of the Oglala Sioux.* Norman: University of Oklahoma Press, 1953.
3. Andrews, Lynn. *Windhorse Woman.* New York: Warner Books, 1989.
4. Andrews, Lynn. *Windhorse Woman.* New York: Warner Books, 1989.
5. The drum is frequently referred to as "the life-force maker" by traditional shamans and medicine people.
6. Ywahoo, Dhyani. *Voices of Our Ancestors: Cherokee Teachings From the Wisdom Fire.* Boston: Shambhala, 1987.

7. Quoted from a speech by John Bourke at the Smithsonian Institution in 1892, in Altman, Marcia; Kubrin, David; Kwasnick, John; and Logan, Tina. "The People's Healers: Healthcare and Class Struggle in the United States in the 19th Century." (Unpublished Manuscript).
8. Campbell, Joseph. *The Flight of the Wild Gander.* South Bend: Regnery/Gateway, Inc., 1979.

Chapter 3: The Fundamentals of Shamanic Drumming

1. Donner, Florinda. *The Witch's Dream.* New York: Simon & Schuster, 1985.
2. Arguelles, Jose. *The Mayan Factor.* Santa Fe: Bear & Company, 1987.

Chapter 4: Power Practice

1. Harner, Michael. *The Way of the Shaman.* New York: Harper and Row, 1980.
2. Ywahoo, Dhyani. *Voices of Our Ancestors: Cherokee Teachings From the Wisdom Fire.* Boston: Shambhala, 1987.
3. Becker, Robert, and Selden, Gary. *The Body Electric: Electromagnetism and the Foundation of Life.* New York: William Morrow and Co. Inc., 1985.
4. Waters, Frank. *Book of the Hopi.* New York: Penguin Books, 1983.
5. Young, Meredith Lady. *Agartha: A Journey to the Stars.* Walpole: Stillpoint Publishing, 1984.

Chapter 5: Healing the Earth

1. Becker, Robert, and Selden, Gary. *The Body Electric: Electromagnetism and the Foundation of Life.* New York: William Morrow and Co. Inc., 1985.
2. Childress, David H., *Anti-Gravity and the World Grid.* Stelle: Adventures Unlimited Press, 1987.
3. Waters, Frank. *Book of the Hopi.* New York: Penguin Books, 1983.
4. Arguelles, Jose. *The Mayan Factor*, Santa Fe: Bear & Company, 1987.
5. Ywahoo, Dhyani. *Voices of Our Ancestors: Cherokee Teachings From the Wisdom Fire.* Boston: Shambhala, 1987.

6. Becker, Robert, and Selden, Gary. *The Body Electric: Electro-magnetism and the Foundation of Life.* New York: William Morrow and Co. Inc., 1985.

Afterword

1. Black Elk, Wallace, and Lyon, William S. *Black Elk: The Sacred Ways of a Lakota.* San Francisco: Harper & Row, 1990.

Appendix B: Chakras

1. Waters, Frank. *Book of the Hopi.* New York: Penguin Books, 1983.

The author is grateful to the following for material reprinted in this book:

Vilmos Dioszegi, for "Shaman's Drum", in "Tuva Shamanism: Intraethic Differences and Interethic Analogies." *Acta Etnographica*, 11:143-190, 1962. Cited in *The Way of the Shaman*, by Michael Harner.

Alfred L. Kroeber, for "Spirit Song" in *Handbook of the Indians of California*. Bureau of American Ethnology Bulletin 78. Washington, 1925.

Washington Matthews, "The Mountain Chant: A Navajo Ceremony", Fifth Annual Report of the Bureau of American Ethnology, pp. 379-467. Washington, 1887.

Knud Rasmussen, for "A Shaman's Magic Song", in *The Netsilik Eskimos: Social Life and Spiritual Culture*. Report of the Fifth Thule Expedition 1921-24, vol. 8, nos. 1-2.

Eva Wilson, for the Mimbres illustrations, courtesy of Dover Publications, Inc.

"Song of the Drum", "Power Song", and "Dreaming the Drum" were composed by Michael Drake.

Index

About the Author

Michael Drake is a writer, teacher, lecturer, and drummer of Cherokee descent. He is a member of the United Lumbee Nation. Through his work, he shares the teachings of both ancient and modern day Earth Keepers. If you would like to write the author, his address is: Michael Drake, C/O Talking Drum Publications, PO Box 1846, Bend, OR 97709. If you wish a reply, please enclose a stamped, self-addressed envelope. Thank you for your interest.

Talking Drum Publications

Special Order Blank

Name: _____

Address: _____

City: _____

State: _____ Zip Code _____

I wish to order the book, The Shamanic Drum: A Guide To Sacred Drumming by Michael Drake. The price is $9.95 per copy (add $2.00 P&H). I understand that I may return the book(s) for a full refund if not satisfied. Please allow four to six weeks for delivery.

	Quantity	Price x Quantity
Mail check or money order to:	_____	$ _____
	Shipping	$ _____
Talking Drum Publications	Total	$ _____
PO Box 1846		
Bend, OR 97709		

This order blank may be photocopied or reproduced for order submission.